Emerging Hispanicized English in the *Nuevo* New South

This volume provides a comprehensive overview of contemporary language shift and identity in a language community in the mid-Atlantic South to offer a unique window into ethnic dialect formation and sociolinguistic processes underpinning dialect acquisition. Drawing on data collected from over 100 interviews of North Carolina Hispanicized English speakers in Durham, North Carolina, the book employs a quantitative approach and uses statistical software in analyzing the data collected to focus on the sociolinguistic variable of past tense unmarking to explore sociolinguistic processes at work in English language learner variation. The focus on a specific variable allows for the opportunity to explore specific processes in more detail, including the ways in which speakers accommodate regional and ethnic varieties of their peers and the internal and environmental factors guiding dialect acquisition. Illuminating new facets to the processes of language learning, language contact, and ethnolect emergence, this volume is key reading for students and researchers in Second Language Acquisition and variationist sociolinguistics.

Erin Callahan is Assistant Professor in the English Department at Western Carolina University, USA.

Routledge Studies in Sociolinguistics

Emerging Hispanicized English in the *Nuevo* New South

Language Variation in a Triethnic Community

Erin Callahan

Routledge
Taylor & Francis Group

LONDON AND NEW YORK

First published 2018 by Routledge

2 Park Square, Milton Park, Abingdon, Oxfordshire OX14 4RN

52 Vanderbilt Avenue, New York, NY 10017

Routledge is an imprint of the Taylor & Francis Group, an informa business

First issued in paperback 2020

Library of Congress Cataloging-in-Publication Data
A catalog record for this book has been requested

ISBN: 978-1-138-06571-0 (hbk)
ISBN: 978-0-367-60713-5 (pbk)

Typeset in Times New Roman
by Apex CoVantage, LLC

For Sabine

Contents

Figures and Tables

Figures

Tables

Acknowledgements

My dissertation committee, who supported the early versions of this work, was made up of some of the most solid people I know. Robin Dodsworth has, very simply, taught me what it means to be a woman in academia. She is one of the hardest-working, most selfless teachers I have ever met; she encouraged me when I didn't realize I needed it and was tough on me when I thought I didn't need it. Erik Thomas took a chance on me and invited me to come do fieldwork in south Texas with him back in 2006 when he barely knew me. He is one of the smartest and most sincere people I know. Dominika Baran has been a consistent source of support and advice, my everyday touchstone and motivator at Duke, and now the author of an inspiring book—and a friend. Julie Tetel and Edna Andrews have advocated for me, both administratively and intellectually, since I came to Duke. Laura Wright is both an honorary linguist and a leader of honor; it was at her urging that I submitted the official proposal for this book. Brent Kinser's professional support has never wavered, up to and during the final hours: he has advised me at every point during the manuscript preparation process. I am very grateful to the anonymous reviewers who read the proposal for this book; their suggestions have made it more comprehensive, coherent and accessible (all remaining errors, of course, are my own). Lori Fernald Khamala has provided me with perspective when I needed it—and a depth of friendship that, I think, few are lucky to have; she's still my hero. Mary Kohn and I have been in the trenches together too many times to count; here's no one else I'd want in my corner, academically or personally. Maribel Rivera: *eres una gran bendición, amiga*. Maryscot Mullins has provided impeccable administrative support that is always underlined by kindness. Katelynn Allmon has both contextualized the undergraduate student experience for me and provided unending day-to-day support. My mother, Karen Callahan, has provided practical support and encouragement underlined by years of experience in early childhood education and birth to kindergarten bilingual settings. Bill Gallagher's presence in my life has been the most welcome kind of surprise, and his personal support continues to sustain me. Karina Vázquez Zazueta (Callahan) is the best sister (the 'in-law' is in name only) an author could ask for—she also provides great translations on demand. Chris Callahan is one of those brothers who "just gets it"—and gets me, as an academic and as a person. Jeff Faulkner has also been a wonderful surprise—and we are lucky to have him by our side. Thanks also to Sashi Rayasam, Alice Anne Kern, Mary Holt and Daniel Isenberg in DPS schools for opening up their classrooms to a bunch of graduate students with record-ers. Even more thanks to the kids at E.K. Powe, Rogers-Herr and Chewning Middle who made this study possible.

Finally: anyone who knows him will tell you that Walt Wolfram will make you a stellar sociolinguist. I could never have predicted the extent to which he would make me a better person.

1 Introduction

The Language of *Marcos*

Marcos:	*I'm more of American than Mexican. I like to eat like, Chinese, Biscuitville, and all that.*
Interviewer [INT]:	*Mm-hm. ¿Y um, que—por qué sientes más americano que mexicano?* (*'And um, what—why do you feel more American than Mexican?'*)
Marcos:	*Because I know more . . . more people recognize me as American than Mexican. And like, I know more English. I know how to read it, speak it, and everything. I don't even know the ABCs in Spanish. That's why.*
INT:	*Pero . . . ¿tienes ganas de aprender español?* (*'But . . . do you want to learn Spanish?'*)
Marcos:	*No.*
INT:	*¿Por qué no?* (*'Why not'?*)
Marcos:	*I just can't. I already try [sic] but I can't. I can't even read the Bible.*

1.1 Overview of the Study

"Marcos" (pseudonym) is a 13-year-old middle school student living in the medium-sized southern city of Durham, NC. He came with his family from the rural state of Michoacán, Mexico, to the US when he was 3-years old. His parents, undocumented immigrants, work as a cook and a house painter in Durham. His favorite hip hop artist is Lil' Wayne. While he claims he "can't learn" Spanish, Marcos later responds to the interviewer's questions in completely fluent spoken Spanish and even scores fairly well on a standardized Spanish academic achievement test, the Woodcock-Johnson (WJ-III) (Schrank et al. 2005). Marcos himself says he "doesn't even know the ABCs in Spanish"—but he is officially classified by the Durham Public School system as an English Language Learner (ELL).

The language of speakers like Marcos is representative of the multifaceted and sometimes self-contradictory set of questions surrounding language shift and identity in the mid-Atlantic South at the turn of the 21st century. What kind of English has Marcos learned—and what kind will he end up speaking? The Southern White Vernacular English (SWVE) of his middle school principal, a middle-aged, male, white Durham native? The African American English (AAE) of a majority of his classmates? Or the 'Spanish-sounding' English of his best friend's younger siblings, some of whom can understand Spanish but can't speak it at all?

This study focuses on the study of language variation and change in southeastern US varieties of Hispanic English (HE):[1] in short, the language of speakers like Marcos. Since the radical increase in in-migration to North Carolina by Hispanic immigrants—394% between 1990 and 2000, and 111% between 2000 and 2010—students from Spanish-speaking countries account for over half of the total enrollment growth in North Carolina Public Schools. Though Hispanic (English-speaking) communities have populated the southwest and western US for generations, the population explosion in the southeastern US gives researchers a window into the first stages of ethnic dialect formation—beginning with second dialect learning and culminating in the construction of a distinct socioethnic variety.

As such, I will examine patterns of English Language Learner (ELL) variation in the speech of a group of HE speakers, in one elementary school and two middle schools, all in Durham, NC. It examines the sociolinguistic variable of past tense unmarking—the occurrence of verb forms that are formally unmarked in past tense contexts where standard varieties of English use simple past forms (e.g., Marcos's response, *I already **try** that* vs. Standard English *I already **tried** that*). By examining patterns in this variable unmarking of tense, the study tests 1) the extent to which English Language Learners are accommodating to the regional and ethnic (AAE and SWVE) varieties of their peers, and 2) which internal/universal factors guide this sociolinguistic process of dialect acquisition, specifically, a) the verb's sound pattern, b) its inherent meaning, or c) the frequency of the verb in the discourse.

1.2   Study Design: Past Tense Unmarking as a Sociolinguistic Variable

The task of a variationist sociolinguistic study is to describe and explain the systematic variation of language structures. Thus, a sociolinguist might study how forms of the verb *to be* are variably deleted in AAE ("She a linguist" vs. "She's a linguist") depending on subject type (full noun vs. pronoun), phonetic environment (preceding consonant vs. preceding vowel) and following grammatical environment (adjective vs. verb). As such, variationist studies begin with a linguistic variable—a specific, quantifiable language structure that seems to act variably in a set of environments (as with the behavior of the verb *to be* in AAE). This study selects unmarked past tense forms (e.g., "I already *try* that") as a variable that consistently appears in the speech of newly arrived immigrants in Durham, North Carolina (NC). Though the acquisition of past tense has been well documented in the SLA literature (Andersen and Shirai 1996), there have not yet been many variationist takes on the process from a sociolinguistic point of view. We have a good idea of how the process may work from a language acquisition standpoint, but not from a social one. Accordingly, the structure is an optimal site for investigating how the process operates sociolinguistically. Do language learners in Durham show the same kind of general effects documented for second-language learners of English in general—specifically more past tense marking in the aspectual classes of so-called achievement and accomplishment verbs—more marking in sentences like *She broke the machine* vs. *When I was growing up, I live in Monterrey*? At the same time, if speakers have contact with speakers of African American English (AAE) and Southern White Vernacular Englishes (SWVE), what effect do the phonological (sound structure) patterns in those varieties have on how speakers develop and produce past tense forms? Specifically, do newly emerging Hispanic English speakers acquire the same kind of consonant cluster reduction patterns documented for these varieties in the variationist literature, where, for example, in AAE, the final [t] of a noun-like form like 'test' gets deleted more often than the [t] in a verb-like form like 'picked,' or more often before another consonant than a vowel or pause ('picked strawberries' vs. 'picked over' or 'the girl that got picked')? Furthermore, what can these linguistic processes tell us about how speakers negotiate their newly forming identities with respect to social categories like language proficiency, age and gender?

Within the context of an emerging ethnolect, a comprehensive exploration of past tense unmarking is especially valuable since the same structure varies in quantifiable ways across multiple linguistic levels—phonology (one regular English tense marker is formed in consonant clusters which are variably reduced according to well-known linguistic constraints), morphology (irregular verbs may be variably unmarked for tense), discourse function (unmarked verbs may have a specific purpose in narratives), language development (increased length of residency (LOR) may affect overall rates) and social function (unmarking and/or cluster reduction may highlight group membership categories in the speech community). In this way, past tense unmarking illustrates both a cross-section of variable processes (i.e., in order to understand how language varies across structural levels) but, in a larger sense, also demonstrates how socially and linguistically situated meanings themselves emerge in the context of the language learner's 'ethnolinguistic repertoire' (Benor 2010); that is, in order to understand how language itself works. What linguistic forms and functions (e.g., phonological vs. narrative variants) stabilize as language learning informs a dynamic process of dialect formation (i.e., as a group's unique, ethnically indexed identity forms in a new community)? Do native and nonnative speakers show the same kinds of same linguistic and social constraints (e.g., is tense unmarking a nonnative effect)? How do these distinctive features enter (and exit) the ethnolinguistic repertoire/grammar over time (i.e., in terms of LOR)? If they do enter the repertoire, how do they (or do they?) demarcate to both insiders and outsiders which speakers are members of the social group?

Data for the project come from fieldwork in 2006 to 2008 funded as part of a National Science Foundation Research Project (BCS-054139) on emerging Hispanic English in North Carolina. I was conducting fieldwork in the three field sites in Durham, NC: E.K. Powe Elementary, Rogers-Herr Middle School and Chewning Middle School. The fieldwork culminated in a collection of 128 bilingual interviews (from a half-hour to an hour and a half in length) with speakers from the Durham site, ranging in age from 3rd grade to 8th grade. A subsample of 42 English language interviews were ultimately coded in terms of a variety linguistic and social factors, including: verb class (e.g., irregular suppletives like *go/went* vs. regular *pick/ picked*); phonological environment (following vowel vs. consonant); lexical aspect (achievement vs. activity); and speaker's length of residency (LOR), gang affiliation, literacy in English vs. Spanish, age, gender and country of origin. Data were then analyzed using statistical programs, including SPSS, and results are presented in graphic form as well as textually. A concluding chapter summarizes trends and suggests areas for future research as well as pedagogical implications for English as a Second/Foreign Language (ESL/ EFL) instructors.

1.3   New Dialect Formation: Contact, Acquisition and Rule Emergence

Variationist sociolinguists—researchers who look at groups of people who vary their sounds, rhythms, word forms and sentences according to the social groups those people belong to—have long looked to language contact to explain the genesis and long-term development of ethnolinguistic varieties in English. In addition to 'traditional' social variables like age, gender (identity), generation, region and social class, etc., a subset of variationists have begun, in the past few decades, to take a longer look at what happens when groups of speakers come into contact (through migration, resettlement, colonization or involuntary occupation) with an entirely new language. This language contact can take place in the speakers' home country when English becomes established as a 'lingua franca' (as with World English varieties in India, Singapore and Nigeria) or when groups of non-English speakers migrate into regions where English is the widely spoken language in society (as with Jewish English in New York City, Chicano English in the US southwest and British Jamaican creole in London). Finally, a special type of language contact, called creole formation, occurs when two groups with no mutually intelligible language come into contact—with one group speaking a prestige variety, the 'superstrate,' and the other a low-prestige variety, the 'substrate.' This is a situation that occurred, for example, during the 16th through the 19th century African diaspora into English-, French- and Dutch-speaking America and the Caribbean. In such situations, a creole is formed with contributions from both the superstrate (typically vocabulary/lexical items) and substrate (typically sound, word and grammar structures), along with universal principles of language organization and adaptation; the resulting linguistic system can vary along a continuum of distinctness from the Standard (European) prestige variety.

This quest to understand how languages and cultures in contact help influence newborn varieties of English has been ongoing for decades—at least, as Trudgill notes (1986: 1) from the time of Uriel Weinreich's seminal 1953 book, *Languages in contact: Findings and problems*. In a rigorous examination of both the linguistic and sociocultural factors affecting language contact, Weinreich spoke of the type of innovations I observed in my fieldwork in Durham:

> Taking its cue from the speech of bilinguals, a language community can, by systematically extending the functions of morphemes in its language, not only change the use of individual forms, but also develop a full new paradigm of obligatory categories on the model of another language.
>
> (Weinreich 1953: 40–41)

As examples of these new obligatory categories, Weinreich gives the examples of constructions formed out of German contact with Polish and Hungarian: Silesian Polish *ja to mam sprzedan* to mean 'I have sold it' (on the basis of the German construction *haben* + past participle), as well as a new Hungarian pluperfect construction using *volt* ('to have') following the past form of the verb (on the basis of the German pluperfect).

In his own contact study, *Dialects in contact*, Trudgill (1986) documents these same kind of innovations after two mutually intelligible English dialects have mixed. In the city of Norwich, England, an urban area that attracted rural newcomers, the pronunciation of 'room' with a vowel more like the sound of American English *eww!* ([ɹʉːm]) has a working-class sounding status, while [ɹuːm], with a vowel like *oo!*, sounds high status). Trudgill catalogs the structural processes that produce linguistic changes in these kind of contact situations, including simplification (an increase in grammatical regularity), leveling (elimination of marked variants), reallocation (redistribution of variants across social categories, including social class) and the creation of interdialect (structurally intermediate) forms (1986: 110–119). He proposes that speakers become more aware of features (i.e., they progress from social indicator to marker) which are 1) overtly valuated, 2) involved in linguistic change, 3) radically phonetically different/distant, and 4) involve phonological contrasts (Trudgill 1986: 11). Crucially, he argues that diffusion of these changes occurs at the level of the individual speaker as s/he comes into contact and talks with others in particular settings. This process of accommodation (Giles 1973; Trudgill 1981), like the modification of non-linguistic behaviors such as body movement, proximity and eye movement, is relatively automatic and unconscious (Trudgill 1986: 2–3). As André Martinet noted in his preface to Weinreich's book, "[c]ontact breeds imitation and imitation breeds linguistic convergence" (1953: viii).

A half decade after the publication of Trudgill's *Dialects in contact*, Chambers (1992) published an influential article in *Language* which built on Trudgill's work on new dialect formation. This eight-stage model predicts that, first, lexical (vocabulary) replacements occur at rapid rate (before phonetic or phonological adaptations), then slow down. Next, simple phonological rules progress faster than complex ones; thus, automatic, categorical processes (like applying T-Voicing[2] in *putting/pudding* and *petal/pedal*) occur before complex ones (like Vowel Backing before voiceless fricatives and /n/ + obstruents, as in *plaster* and *dancing*). Furthermore, the acquisition of these complex rules splits the population into early acquirers and later acquirers, reflecting the broad influence of the critical period.[3] Next, phonological innovations are actuated as pronunciation variants, consistent with a lexical diffusion model (Wang and Cheng 1970; Chen and Wang 1975. Here, a phonological rule springs to life as a speaker encounters it in specific instances (e.g., individual words and sentences); the generalized rule is acquired only after these instances reach a critical mass. At certain stages of acquisition, as learners notice pronunciation patterns in particular words, they hypothesize that these patterns represent an overarching rule. Here, Chambers cites Trudgill (1986: 5) in describing the mechanics of accommodation as a precursor to (long-term) acquisition:

> The point is that during accommodation speakers do not modify their phonological systems, as such. . . . Rather, they modify their pronunciations *of particular words* [his emphasis], in the first instance, with

some *words* being affected before others. Speakers' motivation . . . is phonetic rather than phonological: their purpose is to make individual words sound the same as when they are pronounced by speakers of the target variety.

(Trudgill 1986: 5, cited in Chambers 1992: 694)

In the end stages of Chambers's model, old rules are deleted more quickly than new ones are acquired: the old rules fade away more rapidly than the new rules grow. Next, orthographically aligned variants (like *city*, spelled with <t>, not <d>) are acquired faster than those that are not reflected in spelling (like *summer* spelled with <r> but pronounced without [ɹ] in r-less dialects of English), reflecting the influence of literacy.

A decade later, Schneider (2003) published a comprehensive model of dialect birth by proposing five stages that capture how New English varieties emerge. Within this framework, which focuses on postcolonial settings, Schneider distinguishes between ENL/English as a Native Language countries like Britain, the US or Australia and EFL/English as a Foreign Language countries where English assumes a specialized role in, for instance, fields like business or technology, like Taiwan or Denmark. Finally, English may serve as a widespread 'official' language in multilingual societies in broad areas like politics, jurisdiction and higher education, as in India and Singapore.

In contrast to Trudgill's and, to some degree, Chambers's model, Schneider is more oriented to social identity; his 'theoretical prerequisites' include a recognition of linguistic variability's symbolic function in 'us' vs. 'them' (in-group/out-group) boundaries as speakers confront "a need to decide who one is, and, importantly, who one wishes to be" (2003: 239). One of the important functions of this model is to capture how these changing value orientations and group identities come to evolve via an underlying influence of common historical and sociopsychological processes—in his words, "identity rewritings" (2003: 242). Schneider does recognize that, in the early phases of contact, a structural 'founder effect' (Mufwene 1996, 2001) plays a central role as the linguistic input contains forms from all parties' native languages and varieties competing, as it were, in a pool of possible variants in the emerging variety. Schneider terms these two 'strands' of development the STL strand, referring to the settlers' experience, and the IDG, or indigenous strand. The first phase of this model is FOUNDATION, where English moves into widespread use in a non-English speaking country—for example, because of emigration, colonization or a missionary, military, or trading presence. During this phase, bilingualism spreads in the IDG strand as English ability becomes an advantage in attaining higher social status. The next phase, EXNORMATIZE

STABILIZATION, is perhaps the most applicable to the Durham context. At this point, with some multilingualism established, transfer phenomena begin to hold sway—for instance, via passive familiarity with the L2, code-switching, Second Language Acquisition and 'negotiation': "when speakers their language (A) to approximate what they believe to be patterns of another language or dialect (B)" (Thomason 2001: 142, cited in Schneider 2003: 246). Schenider notes that, during this phase, structural innovations are likely to fly 'under the radar,' probably dismissed by speakers of the prestige variety as errors or 'broken' language since they are restricted to spoken vernaculars. This is a crucial point for sociolinguistic descriptions of dialect emergence, however, since the earliest structural features tied to local usage—'dialect forms' in earnest—begin to occur. While at this stage both IDG and STL group identities remain largely intact (language use does not yet reflect any distinct symbolic function), the raw ingredients for new dialect formation are now present.

During the third phase, STRUCTURAL NATIVIZATION, both groups' traditional social and political perspectives begin to shift and these changing alignments are reflected in language use: in short, both populations realize that their reality is changing; they must learn to 'get along.' This shift is borne primarily by the IDG population, which must undergo broad-based Second Language Acquisition and cultural assimilation. The IDG strand, which may contain elements of substrate influence and interlanguage use, becomes increasingly oriented to the new country, which represents their future. A sociolinguistic continuum forms between conservative users who reject innovations and advanced users who readily incorporate local, sometimes ethnically associated linguistic norms. At this stage, linguistic restructuring gains momentum, as IDG speakers drive the phonological and grammatical changes in the newly emerging dialect; it is here that innovations develop into rules that characterize the new variety. Schneider highlights the lexico-grammatical dimension of this process:

> In descriptive terms, it is interesting that in its early stages of this indigenization of language structure occurs mostly on a lexico-grammatical level, where individual words, typically high-frequency items, adopt characteristic but marked usage and complementation patterns. Grammatical features of New Englishes emerge when idiosyncracies of usage develop into indigenous and innovative patterns and rules. When words cooccur increasingly frequently, locally characteristic collocations and 'lexical bundles' (Biber et al. 1999: 987–1036) will emerge, and in the long run this may result in the development of fixed expressions or idioms. Similarly, grammatical patterns characteristic of one class of words may spread to another word or class of words (most likely

initially in IDG-strand usage, where intuitions as to a pattern's accept-ability are less strictly circumscribed) and become firmly rooted, thus gradually enriching the emerging new variety with additional structural possibilities and ultimately modifying parts of its grammatical makeup (i.e. its lexicogrammatical constraints). Grammatical nativization in New Englishes typically comprises phenomena such as new word-for-mation products (e.g. from South-Asian English *rice-eating ceremony* [Kachru 1986: 41], from Pakistani English *Bhuttocracy, autorickshah lifters*, and so on [Baumgardner 1998] . . . localized set phrases (e.g. the Australianism *no worries*), varying prepositional usage (e.g. *different than/from/to*, known to vary between national varieties of English [Hundt 1998: 105–108], *resemble to* someone) and innovative assign-ments of verb complementation patterns to individual verbs (e.g. *screen* used intransitively and *protest* used with a direct object in NZE [Hundt 1998: 109–112 and 115–118]).

(Schneider 2003: 249)

In the end stages of Schneider's model, the new indigenous variety is widely adopted and a new group identity forms as the orientation to the mother country shifts. Schneider describes a possible 'EVENT X,'

an incident which makes it perfectly clear to the settlers that there is an inverse misrelationship between the (high) importance which they used to place on the mother country and the (considerably lower) importance which the (former) colony is given by the homeland.

(Schneider 2003: 250)

At this point, a new national identity is reflected via the new local norm. In the postcolonial context, the new language variety is now positively viewed as a vehicle for a new regional identity. It may be a first language for some and second language for others, yet is a dynamic variety formed out of built-up interlanguage, substrate and contact features that helps cement the new group's sociopolitical identity. Language shift may occur in earnest, with the L1 endangered or possibly extinct. Codification takes place via dictionary creation and use of the new variety in literary expression. The last phase of the model, DIFFERENTIATION, occurs when dialect emergence is largely com-plete; new regional varieties of the new variety may even emerge. In the ENL contexts named previously, ethnically associated dialects of English may appear; Schneider names Chicano English and Cajun English in the US as two examples.

Finally, Thomason (2001), who is widely cited by Schneider for her empirically based work on language contact dynamics, offers several observations about language contact in the context of interlanguage. In a section on 'imperfect learning'[4] and interference,

> Thomason proposes that as learners import features of the native language, they form a so-called T[arget] L[anguage]$_2$; these features may include 'errors' from the perspective of the (standard)Target Language [TL]. If the TL$_2$ speakers are integrated into the original TL community, they form a hybrid version of the TL and TL$_2$; termed a TL$_3$. This shared variety, which may include borrowed forms from the TL$_2$, is negotiated—probably unconsciously and unintentionally—by speakers of the two groups. By contrast, if the TL$_2$ speakers are not integrated into the original TL community, the TL$_2$ endures asthe group's final TL. Crucially, during this process of imperfect learning, structural interference (in terms of syntax and phonology) precedes lexical interference and also predominates overall. Here, Thomason gives the example of bilingual Yiddish English, which shows moderate lexical interference and strong morphosyntactic and phonological interference. She notes that the degree to which features are integrated into L1—how embedded and intertwined they are with other linguistic components—is one factor that predicts the linguistic outcomes of contact.[5] Here, inflectional morphology is a particularly likely candidate.

In terms of Second Language Acquisition, a more complex type of interference involves projecting L1 structure onto systematic forms in the TL. As an example of this phenomenon, Thomason (2001: 147) points to the development of a so-called second genitive case in one of masculine noun classes of Standard Russian. The Standard Russian structures in this example are 1. the general genitive case (e.g., *cena čaj-a* 'the price of tea[+genitive]') and 2. a partitive genitive construction meaning 'some of' or 'a part of' (*čaška čaj-u* 'a cup of tea[+partitive]'). In the history of Russian, -*a* is the old Proto-Slavic genitive singular suffix for one masculine noun class, while -*u* is the genitive singular suffix for another, smaller masculine noun class. After a period of competition, these two masculine noun classes merged, except in the case of the genitive singular, where both suffixes (1. and 2.) remained, with the special, extra function of partitive genitive for 2. Thomason explains this development in terms of contact and imperfect acquisition. Specifically, as L1 Uralic speakers confronted 2., the 'extra option,' they projected distinctions from their native language (here, the 'empty' genitive and partitive case, with no masculine feature attached) onto the Russian system. She notes that since Uralic lacked noun classes, it would not have occurred to Uralic speakers that the suffixes represented a gender distinction. Instead, the Uralic L1 speakers assumed that the contrasting

Proto-Slavic structures they were acquiring represented familiar functions in their L1, and simply assigned the corresponding familiar functions (general genitive and partitive case) to the contrasting forms in the TL$_2$. I have created the following graphic to represent this process (Figure 1.1):

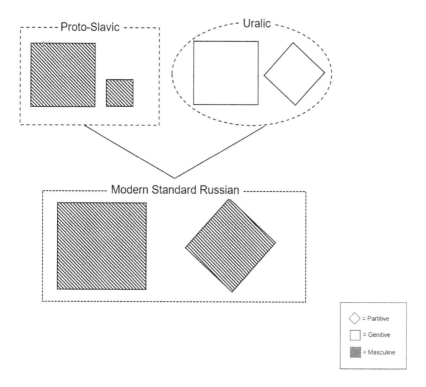

Figure 1.1 Development of Modern Standard Russian partitive genitive

In Chapter 4, we will return to a contextualized discussion of the contact phenomena discussed in this section (functional innovations on the basis of familiar L1 structures, transfer/interference, rule emergence) as well as possible mechanisms for propagation—including individual-level accommodation, lexical diffusion and symbolic function. It is clear that, at most stages of contact, learners have access to a diverse set of structures (both within the L1 and L2) as shared linguistic resources, as well as ongoing interactions with speakers in the new (L2) speech community.

What structures subsequently emerge, how and why is a formidable question. Through an in-depth analysis of one feature, past tense unmarking, in the Durham community, this study will provide one picture of locally specific, quantifiable outcomes in a current triethnic community consisting of Hispanics, white Americans, and African Americans. Here, as a new ethnically associated variety of English emerges, we can ask: what structures and functions survive from the heritage language? What forms do they take in the new variety's sounds, words and sentences? What patterns are discernable to learners across languages/varieties and how/why do these patterns spread?

1.4   A Case Study of 20th Century Biethnic Contact: African American English in Hyde County, NC

If one wishes to examine the weaving of these many strands of contact through history—a dance of categories, behaviors and allegiances forming and re-forming—where to begin? One model, which represents the important contribution of variationism, involves an ongoing strand of research on languages in contact during the African English diaspora (Rickford 1999; Mufwene 2001; Poplack and Tagliamonte 2001). Beginning on the west coast of Africa to the Caribbean and North America, along slave trade routes and the Middle Passage, an array of diasporic African American communities took root as populations of (ex-)slaves and European settlers came into contact. This line of research has investigated the origins and development of present-day varieties of African American English (AAE), among other contact varieties, in terms of links to both colonial British dialects and/or proto-creole origins—as well as 20th-century sociolinguistic settings that reflect both local/regional and supra-regional, ethnolinguistically distinct norms. A key question in these investigations involves the root of ethnolinguistic convergence and divergence from Anglo varieties of English. What role, if any, do West African substrate effects play in forming and maintaining an ethnolinguistic divide? If there are indeed durable substrate effects, what role does language learning play in generating a linguistic 'core' at the heart of ethnically associated, contact-based varieties of English? By contrast, to what degree have African Americans accommodated at various points to the local or regional dialects of their communities—and how/why?

The most meaningful answers to these questions, at least for this author, come from 'going local.' Wolfram and Thomas (2002) address the multiplicity of factors involved in dialect formation and development in a longstanding enclave community of African Americans in Hyde County, North Carolina—a relatively stable, biethnic community in a remote, rural region along the NC coast. The Hyde County sample, which includes 92 African Americans and 52 European Americans born at different points during the 20th century, is used as a case study to investigate the ongoing debate over the origins and development of AAE in the

US. Through an in-depth analysis of well-studied sociolinguistic features in both European American and African American varieties of English, the authors find evidence of 'mixed alignment' across progressive generations of Hyde County speakers. For example, elderly African Americans show alignment to the European American pattern in terms of past tense leveling to *weren't*, a typical regional/Pamlico sound variant (e.g., *I weren't there*), while younger African Americans align to the typical AAE pattern, *wasn't* (e.g., *I wasn't there*). For the feature third person plural *-s* (*The dogs barks at the ducks*), both elderly European Americans and African Americans show usage, but this usage is constrained by different factors (only African Americans use third plural -s with *They* subjects, as in *They barks at the ducks*). Both elderly and younger African Americans show stable patterns of copula deletion, a characteristic AAE feature found in sentences like *She _ nice*. Overall, the authors find considerable intracommunity variation (no one speaker is exactly like another), as well as patterns of correlation (speakers who exhibit high rates of some 'hallmark' AAE feature rank high on others). The overall picture is one of early accommodation to the regional dialect even in the presence of a set of 'core' AAE features, a development that may reflect contact with an earlier AAE creole. Furthermore, Hyde County youngsters seem to be adopting external AAE norms, further widening the ethnolinguistic gap in this community. Wolfram and Thomas locate these patterns of convergence and divergence in terms of sociohistorical events, including US integration after WWII[6] and, in the concomitant period, a growing identification with external AAE norms.

Wolfram (2003) builds on the Hyde County analysis in comparing this community to two other historical enclave communities in NC—Beech Bottom, a small Appalachian community, and Ocracoke, a once-remote barrier island on the NC coast—in order to help chart various patterns of convergence and divergence from regional varieties. All three communities have maintained the long-term coexistence of African Americans and European Americans; however, the communities are sociolinguistically and demographically distinct. On Ocracoke, the lone African American family that remains maintained a variety of English that was subtly distinct for 150 years, despite a lack of contact with mainland African Americans. In Beech Bottom, a tiny mountainous community within the regional Southern Highlands variety, African Americans show higher rates of two features, prevocalic consonant cluster reduction (CCR) and 3rd sg. *-s* marking (Wolfram and Christian 1976; Christian et al. 1989) than the benchmark European American variety—though this difference is receding in the younger generations. On another feature, /ai/ ungliding, African American speech has converged almost entirely with European American speech (both varieties show near-categorical ungilding in the target environments);[7] in fact, in an ethnic identification task, over 90% of Beech Bottom African Americans were identified as white by outsiders in Raleigh, NC (Mallinson and Wolfram 2002). On a morphosyntactic feature, verbal -*s* marking with 3rd pl. subjects (Wolfram and Christian 1976; Christian et al. 1989; Montgomery 1989), Beech Bottom African Americans and European Americans showed similar incidence levels, though these rates were constrained by a subtle grammatical disparity (-*s* marking with collective vs. noncollective nouns and adjacent vs. nonadjacent subjects). In all, these NC African American communities show nuanced patterns of alignment and nonalignment in terms of convergence and divergence from regional (European American) norms. Depending on their demographics, their sociocultural dynamics and their patterns of interaction, African American and European American speakers in these communities both reflect and refract their linguistic histories across time, space and place:

> Although divergence may involve the intensification and, in some cases, innovation of structural traits associated with AAVE (Dayton 1996), it may simultaneously exhibit movement away from localized dialect features as well. In addition, local European American dialect communities may intensify selected features that lead to further separation of African American and European American varieties, as typified by the escalation of past tense *weren't* regularization by younger vernacular Hyde County European Americans. Divergence may, in fact, take several different paths and be bilateral rather than unilateral. It must also be recognized that divergence is not an inevitable path of change for vernacular-speaking African Americans. In Beech Bottom, the few African American speakers appear to be converging rather than diverging over time. Such contrastive trajectories of change suggest that divergence is ultimately embedded in underlying cultural values about identity and is not an inevitable course of change for African Americans.
>
> (Wolfram 2003: 310–311)

1.5 Implications for the Current Study

Having considered these various models for new dialect formation, we can ask several guiding questions: is the emergence of ethnically associated varieties of English due to identity-related factors or mechanistic transmission of substrate-related forms and features—and on what levels, through time and space? In other words, to what degree do contact-related language varieties owe their newborn structure and ongoing development to the straightforward linguistic consequences of contact versus a local/idiosyncratic and social process of group affiliation? If the former (identity-related) explanation is correct, to what degree can we consider these speech forms to be an ethnolect (Clyne 2000) or ethnolinguistic repertoire (Benor 2010)? In the next chapter, we will look at several accounts of the ethnolect as a theoretical construct. These models vary in the degrees to which they assign prominence to linguistic/structural vs. deliberate and performative social processes (e.g., group orientation, individual/agentive stances, identity negotiation). It is hoped that, in this way, we may chart the development of ethnically associated varieties of English through phases of contact, acquisition and (potentially) centuries of development.

Notes

1. The term "Hispanicized English" is used following Walt Wolfram, who notes that "[the term] 'Hispanicized' refers to the contact dynamic with a variety of Spanish influence without a commitment to a resultant ethnic variety, [and] therefore is preferable" (email message to author, February 6, 2017). Here, the focus is on the linguistic processes inherent in the emerging variety, not its particular social meaning in a (regional) community of speakers, for a discussion of issues involved with labeling Spanish-influenced varieties of English in North Carolina. The term 'Hispanic' itself (vs. Latin@/o/a/x or Chicano/a) was chosen because it was the term most frequently used by speakers (in Durham and Granville County, NC schools, during 2002 to 2005, where I worked as a K-12 ESL teacher) to describe themselves.
2. In T-Voicing, a word-medial /t/ is voiced to [d] after vowels and before an unstressed syllable.
3. As Chambers notes, Payne (1980) is striking evidence of this critical period effect on complex phonological rules: early arrivals to King of Prussia (PA) showed an advantage in acquiring the complex Philadelphia short-*a* pattern; crucially, however, no children mastered the rule entirely unless they were the offspring of Philadelphia natives.
4. Thomason emphasizes that 'imperfect learning' does not indicate an inability to learn the Target Language; alternatively, she suggests that "learners must surely decide sometimes, consciously or unconsciously, to use features that are not used by native speakers of the T[arget] L[anguage]" (2001: 74).
5. The other two predictors in this model are universal markedness (so-called marked features that are harder to learn for L2 learners, late to be learned by L1 users, and generally uncommon in the languages of the world) (Thomason 2001: 52) and typological distance between the L1 and TL (the degree to which their structures 'match').
6. The US Civil Rights struggle to end segregation, discrimination and oppression (especially in the US south)—nearly a century after the Emancipation Proclamation—roughly resembles Chambers's (1992) description of an 'EVENT X.'
7. Many varieties of Southern English reduce or monophthongize the /ai/ glide to [a], though it is a particular feature of Southern Highlands English that this reduction takes place regardless of whether the following environment is voiceless (e.g., *tight, rice*) or voiced (e.g., *tide, time*) (Wolfram and Christian 1976).

References

Andersen, R. W., and Y. Shirai. 1996. The primacy of aspect in first and second language acquisition: The pidgin-creole connection. In Ritchie, W. C. and T. K. Bhatia (eds.), *Handbook of second language acquisition*. San Diego, CA: Academic Press.

Baumgardner, R. J. 1998. Word-formation in Pakistani English. *English World-Wide* *19*: 205–246.

Benor, S. B. 2010. Ethnolinguistic repertoire: Shifting the analytic focus in language and ethnicity. *Journal of Sociolinguistics 14.2*: 159–183.

Biber, D., S. Johansson, G. Leech, S. Conrad, and E. Finegan. 1999. *Longman grammar of spoken and written English*. Harlow: Longman.

Chambers, J. K. 1992. Dialect acquisition. *Language 68.4*: 673–705.

Chen, M., and W. Wang. 1975. Sound change: Actuation and implementation. *Language 51.2*: 255–281.

Christian, D., W. Wolfram, and N. Dube. 1989. *Variation and change in geographically isolated communities: Appalachian and Ozark English*. Publication of the American Dialect Society, No. 74. Tuscaloosa, AL: University of Alabama Press.

Clyne, M. 2000. Lingua franca and ethnolects. *Sociolinguistica 14*: 83–89.

Dayton, E. 1996. *Grammatical categories of the verb in African American Vernacular English*. Philadelphia: University of Pennsylvania Dissertation.

Giles, H. 1973. Accent mobility: A model and some data. *Anthropological Linguistics 15*: 87–105.

Hundt, M. 1998. *New Zealand English grammar: Fact or fiction? A corpus-based study in morphosyntactic variation*. Amsterdam: John Benjamins.

Kachru, B. B. 1986. *The alchemy of English: The spread, functions, and models of non-native Englishes*. Chicago: University of Illinois Press.

Mallinson, C., and W. Wolfram. 2002. Dialect accommodation in a bi-ethnic mountain enclave community: More evidence on the development of African American Vernacular English. *Language in Society 31*: 743–775.

Montgomery, M. 1989. The roots of Appalachian English. *English World-Wide 10*: 227–278.

Mufwene, S. S. 1996. The founder principle in creole genesis. *Diachronica 13*: 83–134.

Mufwene, S. S. 2001. *The ecology of language evolution*. Cambridge: Cambridge University Press.

Payne, A. C. 1975. The re-organization of linguistic rules: A preliminary report. *Pennsylvania Working Papers on Linguistic Change and Variation 1–6*. Philadelphia: U.S. Regional Survey.

Poplack, S., and S. Tagliamonte. 2001. *African American English in the diaspora*. Cambridge, MA: Wiley-Blackwell.

Rickford, J. 1999. *African American English: Features, evolution, educational implications*. Malden, MA: Blackwell.

Schneider, E. 2003. The dynamics of New Englishes: From identity construction to dialect birth. *Language 79*: 233–281.

Schrank, F. A., K. S. McGrew, M. L. Ruef, C. G. Alvarado, A. F. Muñoz-Sandoval, and R. W. Woodcock. 2005. *Overview and technical supplement: Batería III Wood-cock-Muñoz: Assessment Service Bulletin No. 1*. Itasca, IL: Riverside Publishing.

Thomason, S. G. 2001. *Language contact: An introduction*. Washington, DC: Georgetown University Press.

Trudgill, P. 1981. Linguistic accommodation: Sociolinguistic observations on a sociopsychological theory. *Parasession on Language and Behavior, Chicago Linguistic Society 17*: 218–237.

Trudgill, P. 1986. *Dialects in contact*. Oxford: Basil Blackwell.

Wang, W. S., and C.-C. Cheng. 1970. Implementation of phonological change: The Shûang-fêng Chinese case. *Chicago Linguistic Society 6*: 552–557.

Weinreich, U. 1953. *Languages in contact: Findings and problems*. New York: Mouton.

Wolfram, W., and E. R. Thomas. 2002. *The development of African American English*. Language in Society 31. Malden, MA: Blackwell.

Wolfram, W. 2003. Reexamining the development of African American English: Evidence from isolated communities. *Language 79.2*: 282–316.

Wolfram, W., and D. Christian. 1976. *Appalachian speech*. Arlington, VA: Center for Applied Linguistics.

2 Why Study Emerging Ethnolects? 21st Century Implications for Variationism and Second Language Acquisition (SLA)

Marisa:	*I'm twelve.*
INT:	*You're twelve. And you're a girl . . . and you were born in Puebla [Mexico].*
Marisa:	*Mm-hm.*
INT:	*And you came to the U.S. when?*
Marisa:	*Like two years ago.*
INT:	*So ten years [in Puebla]. And did you move to North Carolina first?*
Marisa:	*Yes.*
INT:	*Yeah? So, do you have family here- is that why you moved here?*
Marisa:	*Yeah, my dad was here. Well, my dad was here, and he decide to bring us. Because, um- he say that he- he miss us so much when he's here. And we miss him sometimes. 'Cause we are not all together.*
INT:	*How long were you separated- how long was your dad here?*
Marisa:	*Like fourteen- or thirteen years. But my dad go to one year in the- house. But in all the time, it was, uh, thirteen, fourteen years.*
INT:	*Mm. That sounds like it would be hard. What was it like living in Mexico without your dad?*
Marisa:	*Uh- it was like, um- that we don't have dad. We didn't remember who he was so we tell, um, my brothers that are little- we tell him that my dad is in here to work for us. And they say, "okay, and what is his name?" And we have picture of him 'cause, uh, he sent of Mexico. So I tell them, and I show the picture. They say okay.*

2.1 Introduction

This chapter will introduce varying theories of language acquisition in terms of variationist and Second Language Acquisition (SLA) accounts in order to provide a theoretical overview for the quantitative results presented in Chapter 4.

2.2 Variationist Approaches to Interlanguage

Since the publication of Dickerson's 1975 article, "The learner's interlanguage as a system of variable rules," a growing contingent of sociolinguists, trained to analyze (L1) linguistic variation using various quantitative methods, have worked from Selinker's (1972) INTERLANGUAGE model to analyze the speech of second-language learners. These studies have ranged from Dickerson's examination of the variable productions of /r/ for a group of Japanese English Language Learners (ELLs) (Dickerson 1975, 1976) and Bayley's (1991, 1994) study of constraints on the *-t/d* variable in Chinese learners of English to Tarone's work (1979, 1981) on attention and style-shifting in interlanguage systems. These studies have constituted a small but promising foundation for the emerging field of variation in the speech of second-language learners.

In providing a rationale for the existence of this new line of inquiry, Preston writes:

> Since there are probably more bi- and multi-linguals than monolinguals in the world, it should be an idea especially abhorrent to sociolinguists that their special interest can be pursued adequately in ignorance of the messy data produced by such speakers. Many who are known as sociolinguists prefer to be called linguists, assuming that their perspective on language in its broader social context is necessary to any complete understanding not only of the interactional functions but also of the internal make-up of language systems. . . . SLA provides another perspective from which language and its structure may be investigated.
>
> (1989: 2–3)

As a unique kind of speech community, the speech of second-language (or third-language) learners should be a natural object of inquiry for sociolinguists, as well as the kind(s) of competence the knowledge of this speech community represents. The 'messy data' Preston refers to bear more than a passing resemblance to Labov's (1969) earliest data on language variation in the copula, where the systematicity of an individual's speech, unless positioned in the context of a larger speech community, resembled "unaccountable and sporadic variation" (1969: 759). In providing an empirical rationale for the study of variable rules, Labov was, in part, appealing for greater cooperation from the generative community to pursue unified solutions for understanding the nature of variation. To that end, he writes:

> More generally, the paper is directed at the methodological problem which seems to me of overriding importance in linguistics at

the moment: to connect theoretical questions with a large body of inter-subjective evidence which can provide decisive answers to those questions.

(Labov 1969: 757)

A conversation between SLA researchers and sociolinguists would constitute the same kind of methodological advance Labov argues for. While SLA research has typically considered interlanguage variation in terms of a categorical, intuited choice between two forms (frequently, more or less target like), sociolinguists are poised to provide rigorous descriptions of the principled nature of the variation between these forms.

In addition to providing sociolinguists with a unique type of data, second-language learners may ultimately help sociolinguists unify their accounts of synchronic language variation and language change. To the degree that Second Language Acquisition involves the internal development of linguistic systems in the context of the social life— a process manifested in misperceptions, re-balancings, re-evaluations, regularizations, innovations and standard-settings—it may bear fruit for our investigations of socially and linguistically conditioned language change.

To give an example: it was of special importance to sociolinguists to demonstrate, using the construct of APPARENT TIME, that historical processes of language change could be reliably observed in real time. Consequently, sociolinguists are now especially well versed in 'the use of the present to explain the past' (Labov 1963). It is intriguing, then, that the Second Language Acquisition data (e.g., in the form of implicational arrays) have been characterized by some sociolinguists as representing a form of 'violent language change' (see Preston 1989: 32–33). In examining how interlanguage data (especially contact data) 'select' which linguistic tendencies survive into a full-fledged 'ethnolinguistic repertoire' (Benor 2010), we are perhaps at another crossroads where two perspectives may cross in order to address fundamental questions like, "What is the most general form of a linguistic rule?" and, "How do systems of rules change and evolve?" (Labov 1994: 760, cf. Weinreich et al. 1968).[1] In other words, to what degree can an analysis of longitudinal development (in the individual) explicate or model processes of language change (in the speech community)? Or, vice versa, to what degree can variationist constructs designed to explain language change (e.g., real vs. apparent time) account for successive stages in interlanguage development?

This study considers data that come from a privileged window of linguistic time: the stretch between the 'psycholinguistic' process of Second Language Acquisition and the 'sociolinguistic' process of dialect emergence. In exploring how a range of constraining factors—including subtle linguistic and crosslinguistic facts, discourse-level/interactional goals and even developmental universal processes—interact with a single variable, past tense unmarking,[2] in the speech of second-language learners who are also emerging dialect speakers, this study hopes to join the conversations of sociolinguists working on SLA variation, as well as a larger conversation with general linguistic theory.

Wolfram (1990: 105) frames fundamental questions that may need to be answered before any meaningful expedition sets off to chart interlanguage variability:

1. What is the nature of interlanguage variability, both systematic and unsystematic?
2. Beyond simple (correlational) descriptions, can we provide a unitary model that will link description and explanation?

Is all interlanguage variation systematic? Preston (1989) points out that an exhaustive search of factors on variation in a particular environment (linguistic or otherwise)[3] must be carried out before variation can be deemed entirely unsystematic; he is wary of accounts of so-called free variation and writes, "I am suspicious that language variation which is to be influenced by nothing at all is a chimera" (155; see also Preston and Bayley 2009: 99).

Accordingly, there are robust findings in the literature where re-analyses have led to more focused understandings of apparently 'free' variation. Schachter (1986), for example, re-analyzes the variable negation patterns in the speech of a speaker in Cazden et al. (1975): Jorge, a 12-year-old Spanish-speaking student from Colombia. In a longitudinal six-week study that began one month after Jorge entered the US, Schachter finds that both syntactic development (from undifferentiated Eng. *no* + N/V/PP/etc. to elaborated Eng. *no* + N, *not* + V . . .) and functional category (rejection, denial, correction, etc.) systematically constrain Jorge's negation strategies. Schachter emphasizes that the complexity of decisions and procedures of the analyst must match the complexity of the learner's patterns of variation so that "it is the variation itself that should serve as a challenge to further and deeper analysis" (p. 131). Careful analyses like Schacter's provide a rationale for prevailing variationist opinion that 'free variation' usually is not completely free.

On the dissenting side, Ellis (1999 for earlier lists) defines free variation as that which may not be accounted for by a list of five factors:

1. the situational context, covering such factors as the setting and the addressee
2. the illocutionary force of an utterance
3. the linguistic context
4. the discourse context (i.e., the rhetorical mode)
5. the planning conditions under which performance takes place

Ellis argues that the remaining free variation is a product of 'item' vs. 'system learning': acquisition occurs in the context of "loose lexical networks" that are the product of implicit learning: in this context, free variation occurs "when learners add items to those they have already acquired and before they analyze these items and organize them into a system" (1999: 460).

Along these lines, Young (1996) describes free variation as an early stage in the acquisition of English articles by native speakers (NS) of Czech and Slovak learners of English. Here, formal strategies for encoding semantic and discourse information related to reference and topic continuity, which are encoded by different forms in the learners' L1s (for example, via verbal aspect or case marking), are shown to vary according to progressing stages in the interlanguage system. Definite articles show a distinct pattern at the lower proficiency levels, however: they are over-generalized with no clear form-function relation (at least none of those coded in the study). Young notes that this result tallies with similar findings by Huebner (1983) and Chaudron and Parker (1990). Both studies report the same "nonsystematic flooding" of definite articles in the low-proficiency stage of their subject(s): an adult, Hmong-speaking Laotian refugee named Ge and a group of 40 L1 Japanese ELLs. These results lead Young to conclude that free variation of an L2 form may occur under specific conditions:

1. The L2 form does not have a corresponding form in the L1.
2. The L2 form is perceptually salient.
3. There is no clear form-function relation between the L2 form and meaning.[4]
4. Free variation in the L2 form consists of initial overuse of the form.
5. Systematic use of the form begins when the form disappears from some environments.

(1999: 170)

Preston (1989, 1996) is especially candid in criticizing SLA studies that relegate so-called sociolinguistic concerns to only those factors usually within, for example, the ethnography of communication: "[t] hereby, the hard stuff of phonology, morphology, syntax and semantics is avoided; worse, the hard stuff of pragmatics, ethnography, statistics, data collection, and the like is often also not in evidence." Moreover, he isolates one important misunderstanding in the conversation between SLA and sociolinguistics: namely, the former field reduces the concerns of the latter to what might be called "socially sensitive pragmatics" (155).[5]

A passing glance over the literature shows this version of the misunderstanding to be at least somewhat well represented. For example, Oxford (2002: 245–252) describes the goal of her chapter (in an applied linguistics handbook), titled "Sources of Variation in Language Learning," as an essay that will summarize the research on sources of variation in language learning. Oxford's categories include (a) 'large culture' (e.g., individualist vs. collectivist cultures); (b) 'small culture' (autocratic vs. democratic/participatory teaching approaches); (c) second or foreign language learning environment (English learning in the UK vs. English learning in Egypt); (d) stylistic factors (learning styles, personality types); (e) cognitive and affective factors (motivation, anxiety); and (f) demographic factors (gender, age).

Young (1999) notes that approaches like these—including ethnomethodology and conversational analysis—which use preexisting social categories to characterize emergent and dynamic contexts, are widespread in research on sociolinguistics and SLA. Here, fixed factors including gender, age and proficiency are "relevant in understanding a focal instance of language use only to the extent to which participants orient themselves to those categories in interaction" (1999: 106–107). Young characterizes this 'hermeneutic approach' to SLA (Markee 1994) as the framework that has "emerged as the dominant tradition in sociolinguistic research in SLA over the past five years" (1999: 107).

More variationist-oriented approaches to SLA have provided different ways of generalizing the nature of interlanguage variability by proposing factors that tend to be linked either to the linguistic system itself or to the speakers' social situation. This taxonomy has produced the use of terms like VERTICAL vs. HORIZONTAL *variation*), 'individual characteristics' vs. 'interactional factors' (Preston 1989) or 'low-level' vs. 'discourse-level' constraints. Accordingly, two primary volumes on research on variation in second language published in 1987 (eds. Gass, Madden, Preston and Selinker) have the (symmetrical) subtitles *Psycholinguistic issues* and *Discourse and pragmatics*. In the years since the publication of those two volumes, their distinctions have increasingly seemed less useful for the task of providing unified accounts in a workable descriptive model of second-language variation. Tarone (1990) and Young (1999), for example, show the importance of working *across* both 'high-' and 'low-level' sets of constraints. Tarone (1990) investigates task-based variation of four grammatical variables: 3rd person singular -*s*, the article, the noun plural -*s*, and 3rd singular direct object pronouns in L1 Japanese and Arabic interlanguage. Different grammatical forms seemed to show conflicting behavior across tasks that ostensibly required less vs. more attention to form: in the same formal task (a grammar test), noun plural -*s* did not shift; third singular -*s* seemed to increase in accuracy, while articles *decreased* in accuracy. A re-analysis of her original coding scheme, taking into account two new factors, improves the predictiveness of the analysis:

1. the connectedness of the discourse required by the task
2. the communicative pressure brought to bear upon the speaker to be clear in transmitting information

(pp. 11–12)

Tarone notes, for example, that the grammar test, which consists of isolated sentences and thus requires no cohesiveness at all, contrasts in terms of connectedness and communicative pressure (i.e., to be clear) with the narrative task, which requires consistent cohesiveness and a listener with an immediate need for information. The grammatical structures under investigation facilitated this clear communication to various degrees: 3rd singular -*s*, for instance, is usually redundant in terms of coding subject information, while articles (e.g., the choice of *a/an* vs. *the*) provide a rich tapestry of discourse-level meanings related to what is known to the speaker, addressee or both.

In this sense, the Japanese and Arabic speakers formed a single speech community oriented to the same norms: connected discourse when it is required and clear communication when there is a listener involved. In other ways, perhaps linked to transfer, learners from such typologically divergent language groups may constitute distinct, L1-specific speech communities. In this way, Tarone locates patterns of variation located at the individual vs. group level, considered in terms of what kind of speech communities these individuals form within and across language backgrounds (Bayley and Preston 2009).

Preston and Bayley (2009) view interlanguage through the lens of these distinct types of learner speech communities, an approach that may be more workable than a *post-hoc* description of low- vs. high-level factors governing interlanguage variation. This type of reframing may be a familiar reflex, however: processes that were once considered 'external' and 'internal' (competence vs. performance) were unified by descriptions of a speech community, constituted by intersubjective competence, as in New Yorkers' variable productions of /r/ (Labov 1972). With the establishment of these empirical facts, there was no longer such a clean line between the internal and the contextual, between the 'psycholinguistic' and the 'attitudinal,' if productions depended not only on linguistic forms and organization, but social information was linked to those forms.

As such, the role of the group and the individual (and their attendant linguistic systems) has been a proving ground for variationists in the context of its disciplinary trajectory (Wolfram 1969) with respect to more abstract, universalist explanations for the organization of linguistic systems (Chomsky 1965; Pinker 1994), leading to the construction of an 'ideal speaker-listener' as the empirical source for linguistic inquiry (Chomsky 1965: 3–4). What has been convincingly established for NS speech within the variationist paradigm, the central reality of intersubjective knowledge, has not yet been digested by much of the research in SLA, whose focus remains the internal knowledge of an individual language learner. Here, the methodologies for eliciting and analyzing data of SLA and variationist researchers are often mutually exclusive, not simply incompatible. Though there have been relatively more group studies in the last few decades, SLA research has often focused on the learner as an individual—or, in some circles, on the individual learner's 'knowledge' as competence (Tarone 1990).[6] Variationist sociolinguistics, on the other hand, has its origins in large groups of aggregate data from speech communities in large urban centers (Labov et al. 1968; Wolfram 1969). Moreover, Bayley and Preston (2009) point out that a general misunderstanding of sociolinguistics in SLA circles (integrating 'socially sensitive pragmatics' into language learning) often leads to studies where "the hard stuff of phonology, morphology, syntax and semantics is avoided; worse, the hard stuff of pragmatics, ethnography, statistics, data collection and the like is often also not in evidence" (p. 99).

If the role of the individual and the group (i.e., as a Labovian 'speech community' characterized by ordered heterogeneity in not only socially significant meanings and situations but complex linguistic variation in linked forms) is key to bridging the theoretical and methodological gap between variationist sociolinguistics and SLA, then understanding exactly what *kinds* of groups we consider—their composition, the factors that link their members, etc.—is crucial. Preston and Bayley (2009: 101) suggest that a central task of variationists working in SLA is to provide an empirical base for three conditions:

1. All learners from the same language background make up learner communities.
2. All learners from all language backgrounds belong to the same learner community.
3. Subgroups of learners even from the same language background make up distinct communities.

The linguistic correlates of conditions (1), (2) and (3) would be, in terms of interlanguage variation, processes of 1. Transfer, 2. universals and 3. individual variation. How could these conditions be spelled out empirically? In the next section, we will move to an exploration of individual studies using variationist tools to explore multiple independent influences on variable tense marking in second-language speech. This group of studies has helped frame what categories to look for in variation in past tense marking, how to analyze these categories and how an analysis may bridge both multiple linguistic and social levels (i.e., how a variable form operates for learners from different language backgrounds or Lengths of Residency).

2.3   Wolfram et al.'s Vietnamese English (VE) Studies (1980s)

The variationist study of L2 tense marking was initiated by Wolfram et al. (1983) and reported in Wolfram and Hatfield (1984) and Wolfram (1985) in a project that has come to be known as the Vietnamese English (VE) studies. These studies investigated the systematic constraints on tense marking in a Vietnamese community in northern Virginia. The authors used data from 90 sociolinguistic interviews with subjects from four age groups (10–12, 15–18, 20–25 and 35–55) and two length of residency (LOR) groups (a subsection of 32 speakers from the original sample was ultimately used for some analyses). Wolfram (personal communication, 12/14/18) points out that while LOR is conveniently used as a proxy in studies of L2 acquisition, it may in fact be an epiphenomenon for a range of social factors (e.g. L2 proficiency, assimilation). The VE studies explored the influence of eight factors on the shape of morphological tense marking in English:

1. *Regular forms:*

    a. /t/ following voiceless stops, which are not alveolar, as in /mIst/ 'missed' or /kIkt/ 'kicked'
    b. /d/ following voiced stops, which are not alveolar, as in /peyd/ 'paid' or /lind/ 'leaned'
    c. /Id/ following alveolar stops, as in /tritId/ 'treated' or /reydId/ 'raided'

2. *Irregular forms:*

    a. suppletive forms (e.g., *go/went, am/was*)
    b. internal vowel change plus a suffix (e.g., *keep/kept, tell/told*)
    c. internal vowel change (e.g., *come/came, run/ran*)
    d. modals (a special case of internal vowel change and suffix addition: *can/could, will/would*)
    e. replacive final consonants (*have/had, make/made*)

The results demonstrated that both the phonetic composition and the phonological environment of the past tense form systematically affected the relative frequency of marking across both LOR groups. First, regular forms are less likely to be marked than irregular forms, a pattern found in both Second Language (Dulay and Burt 1974; Ellis 1987) and First Language (Brown 1973) Acquisition.

Second, surface unmarking is more likely for forms ending in a phonetic cluster (/mIst/→ [mIs] 'missed' or /kIkt/→ [kIk] 'kicked' as opposed to those ending in a singleton consonant (e.g., /peId/→ [peI] 'paid'). Finally, cluster forms preceding a word that begins with a consonant (e.g., *missed school, kicked people*) are more likely to be unmarked versus those forms which precede a vowel (e.g., *missed autumn, kicked air*). This systematic process of cluster reduction has been widely documented across dialects of English (Wolfram and Fasold 1974; Guy 1980), including Spanish-influenced varieties of Tejano English (Bayley 1994), Los Angeles Chicano English (Santa Ana 1996; Fought 2003) and Puerto Rican English (Wolfram 1974).

Furthermore, the shape of the irregular past tense forms also seemed to constrain marking patterns in a systematic way; this effect also held for both LOR groups. Here, suppletive forms (e.g., *go/went*) are most likely to be marked for past tense and replacive forms (e.g., *have/had, make/made*) are least likely to be marked. Overall, irregular forms (i.e., as a class) were marked more often than regular forms.

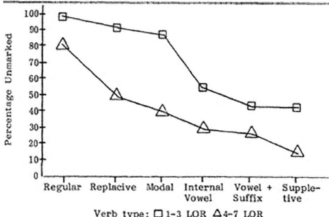

Verb type	Residency			
	1-3 LOR		4-7 LOR	
	No. Unm/Total	% Unm	No. Unm/Total	% Unm
Regular	777/818	95.0	464/584	79.5
Replacive	351/381	92.1	131/255	51.4
Modal	131/158	82.9	53/124	42.7
Internal vowel	495/930	53.2	177/557	31.8
Vowel + suffix	367/824	44.5	151/506	29.8
Suppletive	283/643	44.0	131/760	17.2

Figure 2.1 Incidence of unmarked tense (Unm) for types of irregular verbs, by length of residency (LOR)

Source: Reprinted from Wolfram and Hatfield (1984: 89)

These results are summarized in Figure 2.1 (from Wolfram and Hatfield 1984: 21).

This graph displays the incidence of unmarking based on irregular verb type, where Regular Forms (1a.–c.). > Replacives (2e.) > Modals (2d.) > Internal Vowel Change (2c.) > Internal Vowel Change Plus Suffix (2b.) > Suppletives (2a.). This hierarchy is explained on the basis of the PRINCIPLE OF PERCEPTUAL SALIENCY, in which "the more distant phonetically the past tense irregular form is from the non-past, the more likely it will be marked for tense" (Wolfram 1984: 247).

Though the principle holds reliably at longer LORs, Wolfram notes a strong lexical constraint in the early stages of acquisition.[7] There appears to be considerable individual variation in the rote forms a beginning learner acquires: one learner may acquire marking for the irregular past tense on *go/went* while ignoring *come/came*; another learner may pay attention to marking *come/came* while ignoring *go/went*. Finally, an unrelated type of lexical effect shows up in marking patterns related to relative verb frequency: at particular points during the acquisition process (e.g., internal vowel change for 1–3 LOR group and replacives for 4–7 LOR group), frequently used verbs favor tense marking. Overall, the VE studies do not find substantial evidence for discourse-level constraints operating independent of surface-level linguistic favors.

We will return in section 1.5 to a discussion of how the data from the VE studies fulfill the requirements for Preston's and Bayley's three types of speech communities (described in section 1.1), i.e., how speakers in this study belong to a group of 1) L1 Vietnamese learners of English past tense forms, 2) all learners of English past tense forms and 3) subgroups of L1 Vietnamese learners (e.g., distinguished by proficiency) of English past tense forms.

2.4 The Chinese English Studies (1990s)

Bayley (1994) follows up on the VE studies in a comprehensive analysis of the past tense marking patterns of 20 adult native speakers of Mandarin who are learning English while living in California. Overall, the Chinese English data provide additional (crosslinguistic) evidence for the influence of the principle of saliency in L2 tense-marking patterns, while expanding the analysis to consider additional factors such as grammatical aspect. As we will see, Bayley's studies ultimately provide clues for how to unify our investigations of learner variation through an identification of common linguistic processes and speech communities 1. ((1)–(3)) constituted by one set of L2 speech data.

Speakers in this study were recorded during two sociolinguistic interviews: a one-on-one with the researcher, a non-Chinese native speaker of English, and then in a dyad with another informant. The effects of seven factors on over 5000 tokens were then tested using a VARBRUL analysis:

a. verb type or phonetic form of the past tense
b. the preceding segment (applies only to regular nonsyllabics and some replacives)
c. the following segment (applies to regular nonsyllabics and some replacives)
d. grammatical aspect
e. English proficiency (Test of English as Foreign Language (TOEFL) 550 +, TOEFL 510 -)
f. participation in English-speaking social networks (mixed social network, predominantly or exclusively Chinese social network)
g. interview type (individual, paired)

After collapsing a few of the VE coding categories for verb type,[8] the results confirm the effect of saliency: that is, a greater phonetic difference between a past and present tense form promotes marking of a past-reference verb for tense. Here, only weak syllabics deviate from the saliency hierarchy; this result is explained on the basis of stress: 85% of the regular (cluster) nonsyllabics in the corpus have -t/-d affixed to a stressed syllable, while the -*ed* syllable (as in *wanted*) is always unstressed.

Proficiency level, however, helps sift out some interesting effects. Overall, the ordering of constraints remains relatively stable at higher and lower proficiency levels: the more salient verbs favor marking, while the less salient verbs disfavor marking.

There is an increase in marking overall at the higher proficiency levels; however, these marking patterns do not proceed evenly across verb types. Rather, Bayley notes, "the salient verb types lead" (1994: 172) such that advanced learners mark 80% of suppletives vs. less advanced speakers' 43%, a difference of 37%. The corresponding difference between weak syllabics marked at higher and lower proficiency levels is only 10%. As acquisition proceeds, variability increases across morphological classes, resulting in a greater "spread" for higher proficiency learners who increasingly articulate morphological distinctions in their marking patterns.

In addition to phonetic composition, phonological environment of the verb form also systematically constrains marking patterns. In general, -*t, d* is more likely to be deleted if it is preceded by an obstruent than a liquid or a vowel (*cold vs. las'*); furthermore, deletion occurs on average more often if the following segment is an obstruent or liquid vs. a vowel (*las' night* vs. *last apple*). These patterns are well documented in native varieties of English (Guy 1980; Labov 1989) as well as in the nonnative (VE) data of Wolfram and Hatfield (1984).

Finally, Bayley finds that grammatical aspect strongly constrains marking patterns across morphological classes of verbs, with perfective aspect favoring (factor weight = .68) marking over imperfective aspect (factor weight = .32). As with saliency, this factor seems to constrain the variation learners' interlanguage at a steady rate throughout the acquisition process; perfective verbs favor marking and imperfective verbs discourage it at approximately the same probabilistic weight. In other words, as learners acquire more English, the rule does not disappear in the evolving interlanguage: in fact, as Bayley puts it, advancing speakers simply "turn up the input probability as they move in the direction of target language norms" (1994: 175). This effect holds even when data are reduced to the individual level, such that there is a stable relationship between factor values for perfectives versus input probabilities for 15 speakers in the study.

Furthermore, Bayley observes that the stable influence of perfectivity convincingly recapitulates the behavior of the classic sociolinguistic variable (e.g., (r) in New York City) as described in Labov (1972): here, the aspectual constraint produces a "uniformity of abstract patterns of variation which are invariant in respect to particular levels of usage" (p. 121). In other words, language learners themselves exhibit systematic linguistic variability characteristic of a NS speech community. As such, Bayley argues that the results shown here have two important implications:

> First, the path of acquisition for this feature is tied to markedness. Second, and more interesting, the relatively level influence of past-tense marking according to perfectivity across proficiency levels suggests that no radical restructuring of the grammar as regards this feature has taken place. In other words, although the high-proficiency respondents in this investigation mark more pasts, the probabilistic weight assigned to one of the factors (perfectivity) that significantly influences this marking is nearly equal to the weight assigned the same factor for lower-proficiency speakers from the same group of learners.
>
> (p. 100)

Thus, in addition to confirming the principle of saliency established in the VE studies, Bayley posits that the influence of perfectivity, also stable across proficiencies, may be central (i.e., present across L1s) in accounting for past tense marking patterns.

2.5   Tense Unmarking Studies: The Discourse Rubric

2.5.1   *Foreground vs. Background*

In contrast to variationist analyses, which focus on low-level linguistic factors, a strand of SLA studies has turned to higher-level factors, including discourse constraints, to account for patterns of variability in tense marking for speakers from a variety of source/target language pairs (Larsen-Freeman 1980; Kumpf 1984; Reinhart 1984; Meisel 1987; Véronique 1987; Bardovi-Harlig 1995). This approach assumes that the organization of discourse, typically, but not always, investigated in the context of a narrative (Labov and Waletzky 1967) is the primary motivation for tense alternation in interlanguage speech:

> The assumption is that any grammatical form appears to fulfill a function in the discourse: it is the discourse context which creates the condi-

tions under which the forms appear, and in order to explain the forms, it is necessary to refer to this context.

(Kumpf 1984: 132)

Specifically, these analyses take as primary the division of 'foreground' and 'background' that had been described in functional accounts of grammar (Hopper 1979; Givón 1982). In general terms, background clauses set the scene, change the normal sequence of events, give descriptions, and make evaluations. By contrast, the foreground is the primary event line that advances the storyline as it unfolds: it tells 'what happens next.' Adamson (2009) demonstrates how foreground and background clauses might be identified in a narrative in Figure 2.1:

> Beginning with Kumpf's (1984) study, which examined the speech of Tomiko, a native Japanese-speaking adult, a strand of research in the 1980s examined the extent to which past-tense marking in interlanguage may describe a foreground/background axis rather than a temporal one (Tomiko unmarked tense in all foreground clauses). In a study of native Spanish-speaking students at a middle school in Arizona, Adamson et al. (1996) found evidence that speakers unmarked past tense more frequently in foreground clauses (especially at lower proficiency levels), but noted they did not do so at the dramatic levels of Tomiko.

2.5.2   *Function of the Historical Present in Narratives*

On several levels, which will be explored in this section and the next, the foreground/background account is not as straightforward as it may appear to be. Several authors have pointed out wrinkles in the new discourse-level overlay.

First, Wolfson (1982) argues that NS intuitions for temporal reference may not capture the rules that nonnative speakers use in narrative discourse. She elaborates on the use of the conversational historical present (CHP) as a sociolinguistic (interactional/discourse-level) variable that alternates depending on constraints in the speech situation, as well as a textual device for organizing the (native) speaker's narrative, specifically, the separate episodes in the storyline from one another. Following Godfrey (1980), and working within the narrative framework provided by Labov and Waletzky (1967), Wolfson argues for

> the pattern past-CHP-past with the partition of events being defined by the switch in verb tense such that the most dramatic point is signaled by a switch to the past tense.

(1982: 63)

Wolfson illustrates this function with the following excerpt from her data, a "fight story" recounted by a teenaged speaker of African American English. The italics are in the original excerpt; CHP is underlined here for convenience:

M: "You know why they jumped him?"

P: "Well, you see there *was* a Lincoln boy and a Snyder boy *got* in a fight. And Benny *was* about my height. And Benny *ran* and he *grabbed* the two and he *pulled* them apart. And, like he *got* them both. And like the Snyder boy *started* to hit Benny and Benny *pushed* him back and he *fell* on the ground. And the dude from Lincoln just *stand*[9] there and *looked* at him because he *know* how Benny is. So um, Benny <u>*lets*</u> him go and Benny <u>*turns*</u> around and <u>*says*</u>, 'Why you wanna do that?' And when Benny *said* that, all the other dudes just *jumped*. Well, when they *jumped*, they just, all the other kids *torn* them off Benny. Like see, Benny *recognized* most of the kids that *was* on him, *hitting* him. And like Benny just *went* out and *got* his brothers and that *was* it that night.

Here, CHP serves the function of bringing the dramatic climax of the narrative ("Benny lets him go and Benny turns around and says") to the forefront of the interaction in terms of a temporal shift in morphology.

In order to consider the effects of these types of episode boundaries, Wolfram (1984) re-tabulates representative data from one speaker in his VE study. He finds a few cases that support switches at episode boundaries but concludes on the basis of more prominent low-level patterns (e.g., consistent unmarking of *have* and *go*; consistent marking of *come* and *do/don't*) that a consideration of the surface constraints is critical when examining tense alternations.

2.6 Tense Unmarking Studies: The Role of (Two Kinds of) Aspect

The acquisition of tense and aspect has been an active, contentious area of research in both First Language Acquisition as well as SLA. In this section, a discussion of that debate will bring the issues into contact with findings on interlanguage tense/aspect in the variationist literature. More specifically, we will consider which aspectual meanings overlay the constraints proposed so far in variationist studies (i.e., are ultimately isomorphic) and, by contrast, which distinct meanings/constraints may emerge (or be usefully recast) by looking across disciplines.

2.6.1 *Semantic/Lexical Constraints: Akionsart*

Vendler (1967) classified verbs on the basis of lexical aspect, or *akionsart*, an inherent property of their meaning, proposing a four-way taxonomy. This type of aspect has also been called "situational aspect." Verbs (and sometimes their predicates) fall into distinct categories according to aspect: STATES, ACTIVTIES, ACCOMPLISHMENTS, AND ACHIEVEMENTS. These categories may be further sorted by which semantic features attach to each classification: stative verbs (*like, think, have*), for example, have no endpoint: they are STATIC (vs. DYNAMIC). Activity (or unbounded) verbs (*walk, drive, swim*) have duration; however, they are temporally homogenous: they have no natural endpoint in time that logically defines them. Accomplishment (or bounded) verbs (*make* (a speech), *build* (a house), *run* (a mile)), however, have a necessary endpoint: they are TELIC, as opposed to activities which are ATELTIC. Finally, achievement verbs (*arrive, find, die*) differ from all three previous types in that they are PUNCTUAL or instantaneous: at the moment they occur, the action to which they refer is finished. As such, they have a natural endpoint: like accomplishments, they are necessarily telic.

Vendler provides several tests for each kind of classification: the basic meanings of activity and accomplishment verbs, for example, may occur in imperatives (e.g., *Run! Run a mile to the store!*) while stative and achievement verb meanings cannot (**Know the answer!* *Happen!*)

In both the L1 and L2 acquisition, it is consistently observed that speakers sometimes mark aspectual designations over temporal reference in the early stages of development (Antinucci and Miller 1976; Bloom et al. 1980; Weist et al. 1984; Slobin 1985; Andersen 1989, 1991; Shirai and Andersen 1995; see Andersen and Shirai 1996; see Bardovi-Harlig 1995 for a review). De Villiers and de Villiers (1985), for example, found that in the early stages children acquiring English used the past tense to mark perfective and punctual actions; similar findings have been produced for French (Bronckart and Sinclair 1973) and Modern Greek (Stephany 1981). SLA research has tested this claim, termed the PRIMACY OF ASPECT HYPOTHESIS (POA) across a variety of L1/L2 typologies, including Russian- (Flashner 1989) and Spanish-speaking (Robison 1990, 1995) learners of English, as well as Chinese learners of Japanese (Shirai and Kurono 1998). Accordingly, Bardovi-Harlig and Bergström (1996) argue that the developmental sequence, in which past tense marking begins with achievement and accomplishment verbs and progressive starts with activity verbs, is becoming established as a universal in SLA research.

2.6.2   *Grammatical Constraints: Point-of-View Aspect*

As opposed to lexical aspect, which is tied inherently to the verb's meaning, grammatical aspect describes a particular speaker's point-of-view on a specific event described in a sentence (or text).[10] Comrie (1976) describes

Table 2.1 Semantic features for Vendler's (1967) four event classes

	State	*Activity*	*Accomplishment*	*Achievement*
Punctual	–	–	–	+
Telic	–	–	+	+
Dynamic	–	+	+	+
	Know	*Run*	*Run (a Mile)*	*Arrive*

this function as different ways of "viewing the internal temporal consistency of a situation" (p. 3): in English, for example, a speaker may view an event in its entirety as a single whole (perfective aspect: *She had lunch*) or, alternately, may attend to the internal structure of an event (imperfective aspect: *She was having lunch*). The imperfect-preterit distinction is morphologized in many languages, such as French, Spanish, Russian, Modern Greek and Persian.

Comrie's (1976) binary features constituting to grammatical aspect are mapped on to Vendler's four-way classification schema for lexical aspect in Table 2.1.

As mentioned in section 2.4, Bayley (1994) tested the perfective-imperfective aspectual opposition for L1 Mandarin learners of English. He noted that Chinese grammaticalizes aspectual distinctions over tense, marking the perfective with the clitic particle *-le*. Bayley concludes that marking patterns in Chinese English interlanguage, where perfective aspect favors marking, are the result of the convergence of two processes: 1. *a typological universal* (single, completed events will prototypically occur in the past) and 2. *transfer* from the first-language aspectual system (which marks perfective with *-le*).

Bayley's analysis is in line with Andersen's and Shirai's (1994, 1996) influential PROTOTYPE account, which addresses the POA hypothesis by proposing that "children acquire a linguistic category starting with the prototype of the category, and later expand its application to less prototypical cases" (p. 758). Andersen and Shirai try to account for the (sometimes conflicting) observations in the SLA literature related to lexical and grammatical aspect, as well as foregrounding and backgrounding functions in interlanguage speech, by relating aspectual meanings to prototypical characteristics of 'past-ness' (including, for example, telicity).

The speakers in the first prototype studies (re-analyses of the speech of Brown (1973)'s Adam, Eve and Naomi) initially mark past morphology with instances of [+punctual], [+telic], and [+result] verbs, as well as gradually extend past inflections to other peripheral/non-prototypical verbs.

Furthermore, a distributional bias (in the direction of prototype features, though not reaching the levels of the children's marking patterns) is noted in the input, the native speech of the children's mothers (Table 2.4).

The prototype analysis is attractive in unifying discourse-level (narrative) functions such as foregrounding and backgrounding with the optimal kinds of semantic and grammatical 'tools' speakers (both native and nonnative) have to code these functions. In addition to the explanation for foreground and backgrounding, it brings together many of the important observations noted in the previous sections, including 1) the stable influence of perfectivity (cf. Callahan 2008) and 2) Andersen's and Shirai's (1994) comment on the role of frequency on past tense marking patterns:

> It is almost commonsensical to observe that learners cannot learn everything simultaneously and instantly. In the realm of tense and aspect marking, it appears that what they first learn are the basic tools they will continue to use later as more fluent speakers. We contend that learners are motivated by the same communicative need to distinguish central events (with past/perfective marking from simultaneous situations (with progressive) and both from static background (initially with present verb forms, much later with past imperfectives, or, for languages like English, with past habitual *would/ used* to). Furthermore, as learners acquire more of the linguistic repertoire they need to use the language they are acquiring, they elaborate on this basic framework rather than abandoning it.
>
> (p. 153)

This analysis becomes more attractive in accounting for several other recent findings that are relevant to variationist work on interlanguage. First, the prototype account has been applied to the tense-aspect systems of creoles, which tend to have an overt imperfective or progressive marker, and encode perfective or nonprogressive with zero (Bickerton 1981; Shirai and Andersen 1995; Poplack and Tagliamonte 2001). Andersen and Shirai (1994: 760) also note that, in language change, past tense and perfective morphology have been documented to have developed from [+resultative] and [+perfect] aspect markers in languages of the world (Bybee and Dahl 1989; Bybee et al. 1994).

Finally, Bayley (1999) and Schecter and Bayley (2002) extend the POA hypothesis to communities undergoing language shift, as from Spanish (/English bilingualism) to English in south Texas. In a study of 27 elicited narratives from children aged 4–12, Bayley investigates the extent to which loss of tense/aspect forms mirror the language acquisition of L2 (Anglo) learners of Spanish. He finds that the prototype account predicts how morphological distinctions may be lost during the process of language shift. Specifically, there is an implicational relationship for the order in which non-prototypical aspectual forms lose their past-tense marking: for speakers with high Spanish proficiency, all aspectual forms are marked. However, for individuals who lead language shift/loss, only punctuals are marked by preterit and statives by imperfect (the reverse order in which these forms are acquired).

2.7   Next Steps

In looking towards the future, Wolfram (1978: 19) argued that similar systems of structured, inherent variability exist in both 'sociolects' of NS speech and in the interlanguage systems of language learners. Within both systems, he hypothesized:

> there is a patterned relationship in which certain variants are clearly favored over other variants depending on the context. And although there may be important nonlinguistic variables that influence relationships of *more* and *less* (e.g. stage of second language acquisition), there also is evidence for the existence of independent linguistic constraints on variability (e.g. environment).
>
> Wolfram (1978: 19)

Wolfram's hypotheses have borne fruit in our evolving understanding of tense/aspect interlanguage variation. Specific developments include:

1. Unified accounts of tense and aspect marking for native and NS speakers, specifically, those accounts (including POA and prototype models) that also capture processes in discourse structure (foregrounding/backgrounding), creolization, language change and language shift.
2. The role of converging linguistic factors at the phonetic, morphological and phonological levels of L1 and L2 speech, including the PRINCIPLE OF PERCEPTUAL SALIENCY (see section 2.3).
3. The nature of interlanguage variation located at the individual and group level, especially in terms of what kinds of speech communities these individuals form within and across language backgrounds.

In the 30 years since Wolfram's predictions, in fits and spurts, SLA and (variationist) sociolinguistics have begun to glance across the Saussurian divide: to begin to provide converging accounts of social and psycholinguistic processes in both First and Second Language Acquisition (Preston 1989, 1996). In important ways, this convergence has occurred to the extent that 1) variationists were able to join larger disciplinary conversations on a cognitive capacity for language-making and 2) SLA researchers were able to compromise on their categorical intuitions and peremptory conditions in favor of empirical facts for describing the language usage of real people living in communities in time and space.

Along these lines, Wolfram concludes:

> I am convinced that many of the questions about linguistics in general and contrastive linguistics in particular will not be answered until we look at language *in terms of its actual usage* rather than some idealized construct of how we expect it to work *prima facie.* [my emphasis]
>
> (1978: 25)

It is hoped that the present study, an account of interlanguage past tense marking in the emerging Hispanic English of one community in North Carolina, will continue the productive, cross-disciplinary conversation between variationists and researchers in SLA.

2.8   Variationist Sociolinguistics: Quantitative Traditions

In this section, I will provide an overview of some of the assumptions and methodologies used in quantitative variationist (socio)linguistics, beginning with classical variable rules and ending with contemporary questions of how to best hypothesize about, code and analyze grammatical variation in the ethnolect. A familiarity with these principles will allow the reader to understand the rationale for general design of this study, including coding decisions and presentation of results (Chapter 4), relevance of the results in the triethnic community context (Chapter 3) and broader applications for the general findings (Chapter 5). Ultimately, along with the presentation of results in Chapter 4, I hope to establish some of the ways in which variationist methodological practice establishes and reifies assumptions in terms of core disciplinary constructs (e.g., formal variable rules, VARBRUL 'factor groups') and how a shift to more recent techniques and models (comprehensive statistical programs, usage-based approaches) can determine how methodology itself dictates the kind of results we find.

2.8.1   The Sociolinguistic Variable

Traditionally, variationists have studied how language structures vary systematically at various levels of linguistic organization (for example, the syntactic, phonological or lexical level). The task of a variationist typically

involves isolating a language structure (termed a linguistic variable), iden-
tifying variants of the variables, and investigating how the variants of the
structure patterns across different social categories (region, age, class)
and in different linguistic environments (a verb that occurs habitually vs.
nonhabitually):

1. The term 'pail' vs. 'bucket' for northern vs. southern regions of the US.
    (Kurath 1949)

2. The pronunciation *singing* [ŋ] vs. *singin'* [n] for 'model' vs. 'typical'
    school-aged boys in New England.
    (Fischer 1958)

3. The use of invariant 'be' in sentences like *He be tired* (vs. *He tired*) in
    working-class vs. middle-class African American Detroit.
    (Wolfram 1969)

The examples in 1.–3. illustrate what laypeople tend to think of as 'dialect'
or 'vernacular' forms of English, or what linguists describe as examples of
language variation.[11]

Along these lines, section 2.8.2 will provide a case study of a classic
linguistic variable that has been widely studied in variationist sociolinguistics, namely consonant cluster reduction (CCR), in order to illustrate
this complexity of dialect patterning as well as demonstrate the kinds
of nuanced social effects these patterns have established in the first
few decades of variationist research. After laying this groundwork, sections 2.8.3–2.8.5 will extend these earlier methods and assumptions in
order to discuss contemporary methods and paradigms for quantitative
sociolinguistics.

2.8.2 Case Study: CCR Across English Varieties

In addition to copula deletion, a diagnostic case of variability that has been
studied extensively over the last four decades is the phenomenon of consonant cluster reduction (CCR). This process occurs when syllable-final
consonant clusters, usually both unvoiced ([st] as in 'test') or both voiced
([nd] as in 'friend'), the second of which is a stop consonant, become
reduced to only the initial segment (*tes'*, *frien'*). This variable is especially
useful to consider in the context of the present study since its investigation
serves a dual purpose. First, as a "paradigm case of systematic variability in variation analysis" (Wolfram et al. 2000), the functioning of CCR
illuminates much about the principles and methods of the field of variationist sociolinguistics on the whole. Second, as a phonological process,

CCR is directly relevant to the grammatical process of tense unmarking since one class of regular English past tense forms ([pIkt] 'pic*ked*,' [lind], 'lea*ned*') are formed in a final consonant clusters. Thus, the unmarking variable (*pick*—>[pIk]; *lean*—>[lind]) for verbal tokens in the Durham data may be due to phonological reduction in conjunction with, or in the absence of, other structural factors (verb class: regular vs. irregular verb), usage-based effects (frequency of the word in discourse) or developmental influence (proficiency in English/LOR).

In fact, as a language transfer feature, CCR has had an important role in helping researchers understand the development of various ethnic dialects of English through history, including African American Englishes (West African substrate), American Indian Englishes (indigenous American substrate) and Latino/Chicano Englishes in the southwest US (Spanish substrate). These varieties sprang from ancestral languages lacking syllable-coda consonant clusters and the resulting systems exhibit high rates of CCR due to transfer effects. In the Wolfram et al. (2000) study of the Lumbee Indians, who have lived in tri-racial Robeson County, NC (along with African Americans and Anglo American) for centuries, high rates of CCR may indicate that a source language lacking consonant clusters forms a backbone for this group's ethnic variety of English. Though the Lumbee no longer possess an ancestral language (and have, in fact, struggled for federal recognition as a Native American tribe), the CCR in its present-day variety illustrates how contact effects can endure long term—even in monolingual varieties of English.

While highlighting its contact history, CCR can also point the way towards an ethnic dialect's future. As an ethnolinguistic marker, CCR can vary according to social factors like ethnicity, social class, gender, social networks and peer groups.

While it has been established that even formal registers of very standardized English frequently delete consonant clusters preconsonantally ([pIk] *through* for 'picked' through), levels of CCR across varieties dip precipitously if the cluster occurs before a vowel (*pick up* for 'picked up') or, as in the unmarking of verbs, as part of the morpheme that forms the regular English past tense marker -*ed* (*picked through/up*).

The reliable effects of phonological environment (prevocalic vs. preconsonantal) as well morphemic status (whether the cluster encodes a distinct meaning, as in the bimorphemic token *leaned/lean'* + *ed* but not the monomorpheme *sand*[12]) across register, social class, region and ethnicity have established CCR as a hallmark sociolinguistic variable that can reliably demonstrate nuanced social effects (Labov et al. 1968; Fasold 1972; Wolfram and Christian 1976).

In addition to broad demographic categories like ethnicity, region and class, CCR was shown early on to demonstrate finer-grained local distinctions. For example, Labov (1972), in a study of the speech of adolescent male street gangs in Harlem, New York, illustrates how CCR can help delineate social networks in terms of gang affiliation. Here, not only the overall frequency of CCR rule application across constraints (phonological environment, morphemic status) but the rank orders of these constraints illustrated complex facts about social organization. In Labov's study, the primary constraint on CCR among gang members was following phonological environment (consonants promote reduction) while morphemic status was secondary (monomorphemes promote reduction) for 'lames,' or individuals without strong gang.

In fact, for CCR, a full range of linguistic/internal constraints function consistently across varieties of English (Wolfram et al. 2000). The following list summarizes these findings:

Following Context

preobstruent > presonorant > prevocalic
(e.g., [bEs kId] 'best kid' > [bEs nem] 'best name' > [bEs at] 'best at')

Preceding Context

nasal > lateral > sibilant > stop
(e.g., [wIn] 'wind' > [waIl] 'wild' > [wEs] 'west' > [ak] 'act')

Morphological Marking

monomorphemic > redundant bimorphemic > bimorphemic (e.g., [gɛs]
   'guest' > [slɛp] 'slept' > [gɛs] 'guessed') Stress [—stress] > [+stress]
(e.g., ['kantræk] 'cóntract' > [kan'træk] 'contráct'

Social Factors

lower social status > higher social status casual style > formal style
   AAVE > Anglo vernacular varieties
Hispanicized Vernacular English > Anglo vernacular varieties Vietnamese English > Anglo vernacular varieties

I have examined how CCR may occur at higher rates overall before a consonant as well as when it does not encode a stand-alone meaning, as in bimorphemic tokens in which the cluster marks past tense (e.g., 'mist' > 'missed'). The list shows how these constraints pattern on an even finer level, introducing the intermediate level of 'redundant bimorphemic' environments like sle[pt], where the cluster carries redundant information about past tense marking that is also signaled by a vowel change ([slip] 'sl*ee*p' [slɛpt] 'sl*e*pt'). Even further, we can observe finer-grained phonetic distinctions: beyond sensitivity to the broad categories 'vowel' and 'consonant,' CCR patterns are predictable for subcategories like a preceding nasal [wɪn] 'win' vs. stop [æk]. Another group of internal constraints appears at the linguistic level of syllable stress, where unstressed syllables (as in ['kantræk] 'cóntract') promote reduction over stressed syllables (as in [kan'træk] 'contráct').

2.8.3　VARBRUL

After the initial introduction of variable rules, a statistical analysis program called VARBRUL (Cedergren and Sankoff 1974) was developed to calculate probabilities, called factor weights, at a greater level of sophistication for linguistic data. Specifically, VARBRUL calculates a factor weight, or probability score (p), that predicts whether a variable rule will be applied: a value above 0.50 indicates that the factor promotes the rule and a factor weight below 0.50 indicates that the factor inhibits the rule. Another VARBRUL measure, the input probability, indicates the baseline probability that the rule will operate independently of any of the constraints under investigation (i.e., an overall tendency).

Factor weights allowed variationists not only to rank constraints (e.g., C > V) but also to compare the relative *strength* of factor weights among and across factors. In addition to the input probability, two other important values are associated with a VARBRUL analysis: the total chi-square and average chi-square per cell. The former value allows the researcher to assess the degree to which the factors function independently of each other: a higher score indicates the factors are significantly correlated with each other (for example, syllable stress is correlated with an upcoming pause vs. an upcoming consonant). Average chi-square per cell gives the researcher an indication of the model's explanatory power: the lower this value (with a maximum of 1), the more indication that the model comprehensively accounts for the variation observed for the study variable in a given data set.[13] Finally, as a stepwise regression procedure, VARBRUL adds in factor groups incrementally in order to assess the unique contribution of each group; factor groups that do not show significant correlations with the dependent variable are discarded from the model.

In all, VARBRUL represented a significant empirical advance over classical variable rules in that it allowed researchers to establish the significance of factors on variation as well as examine the probabilistic strength of those factors and, to a lesser degree, the relative independence of factors (for example, in the form of total chi-square or factors that were dropped from the stepwise model). Practically speaking, factor weights and factor groups were convenient standards that could be referred to across studies and the program itself was relatively accessible for new users. For these reasons, VARBRUL became the 'Gold Standard' (Guy 1980) for measuring categorical variation well into the 21st century.

2.8.4   Quantitative Analysis Post-VARBRUL

VARBRUL has faced increasingly focused criticism in the last decade, some of it centered around the fact that it is not a suitable tool for testing interactions among factors. Furthermore, though it can be demonstrated that in some cases individual data does in fact reliably articulate group patterns, both in native speaker variation (Guy 1980) and in SLA (Bayley 1994; Bayley and Langman 2004), the question of individual-level effects is not readily accessible when using VARBRUL to address aggregate data (though each individual speaker's data could, in theory, be entered individually). In a broader way, the debate over the quantitative sufficiency of VARBRUL spells out the evolution of contemporary questions in variationism: whereas an earlier tradition referred to static 'features' like CCR (or copula absence), more recent research has demonstrated the ways in which categorical variation may ultimately show continuous type effects, most vividly in terms of word frequency and patterns of actual usage.

2.8.5   The Lexical Dimension of Diffusion
and Low-Level Rules: Frequency

Bybee (2000b, 2002) presents evidence that CCR is in fact not an abrupt process, but lexically gradual, as it is mediated by actual usage patterns; under this view, there is an overall 'input value' not only for the phenomenon as a whole, but for each individual lexical item (or combination of lexical items). This set of experiences by the speaker/listener is (cognitively) stored in the form of exemplars (Bybee 2000a, 2001; Johnson 2001; Pierrehumbert 2001) that show association across multiple linguistic levels (e.g., phonological, morphological and semantic similarity) and are strengthened with repeated exposure and use (including face-to-face interaction). In his study of dialect mixing and diffusion, as well as accommodation, Trudgill (1986: 24–28) notes that lexical accommodation can in fact precede morphological or phonological effects, as lexical differences are both highly salient and highly accessible (i.e., they are mostly nonsystematic items able to be learned one at a time); as evidence of the regularity of this accommodation process, he cites a study of Swedish women living in Norway who follow a "regular and common route" towards long-term accommodation of Norwegian (Nordenstam 1979).

In a re-analysis of Santa Ana's (1991) Los Angeles Chicano English CCR data, Bybee (2000b) first demonstrates that high-frequency words[14] do exhibit CCR at significantly higher rates overall (54.4% vs. 34.4% reduction; $\chi^2 = 41.67$, p < .0001). Bybee (2002) then extends this account by introducing evidence that bears directly on our investigation of CCR in the context of marking a morphological distinction (regular English past tense *-ed*). Specifically, she shows that regular past tense forms occurred before vowels at a high rate (40% vs. 21% for the overall corpus) and argues that it is the frequency of the prevocalic occurrence that conditioned retention, not morphological status as such. Thus, words that occur more frequently in a phonetic context favoring reduction undergo the variable process at a higher rate than those that do not frequently occur in the favorable context. This analysis represents a fundamental shift from the 'functional load' paradigm (Kiparsky 1972) in positing actual contexts of (phonetic) use in over abstract morphological information ('bimorphemic' vs. 'monomorphemic' tokens).

Bybee's results for CCR reflect a larger debate on the role of lexical diffusion and frequency in variationist sociolinguistics—whether the word or the sound is the fundamental unit of linguistic variation and change (Wang and Cheng 1977; Phillips 1980; Labov 1989; Labov 2010) and, consequently, how this question can be squared with traditional modes of analysis that rely on structurally specified (VARBRUL-type) factor groups. We will address these questions empirically in the presentation of the quantitative results of unmarked tense patterns in the Durham (HE and AAE) speech community. For example, section 5.3 will outline decisions that must be made in coding and quantifying frequency in studies of grammatical variation, including whether frequency should be treated as a traditional 'factor group' at all, or one which intersects in complex ways with structural categories (Poplack 2001; Erker and Guy 2012). Chapter 5, which includes a discussion of HE in the community context, will return to this question of usage-based effects, specifically in terms of the structural categories morphemic status and phonological environment, as well as their collinearity with respect to frequency.

Notes

1. Labov (1994: 760) also pointedly asks (in the same series of questions), "How do languages, originally diverse, combine within a bilingual speech community?"
2. I originally chose the term 'unmarking' (vs. 'lack of past tense marking,' etc.) to remain consistent with Wolfram and Christian's Vietnamese English studies, one of the first to examine past tense marking in interlanguage. I do not mean to

suggest that speakers are removing marking in some way, only that (in a descriptive sense) the verb forms are not overtly marked for Standard English type past tense.

3. Preston's (1989: 194–238) impressive taxonomy includes '50-some-odd' factors of 'sociolinguistic concern,' including linguistic, individual, interactive and sociological processes relevant to the study of language variation.

4. Presumably, this set of factors would apply only to cases of free variation of elements in the L2 morphosyntactic system.

5. Preston (1989), however, explicitly notes that to draw analytic brush strokes in terms of individuals vs. interactions is arbitrary; indeed, "[a]s interrelated variables multiply, it will become as difficult to refer back to some as it would have been to exclude them at an earlier stage of consideration. Perhaps only the fact that interactions are made up of individuals suggests this order" (53).

6. It has been shown in SLA studies, of course, that individuals can have widely different routes to proficiency, to say nothing of their idiosyncratic strategies for voicing 'styles and selves.' These concerns are set aside for now.

7. Wolfram et al. (2000) also highlight the role of the frequent lexical items in the early stages of acquiring phonetic processes: in their study of emerging Hispanic communities in North Carolina, they note "some speakers may acquire a glide-reduced production of the /aɪ/ vowel in the lexical item *Carolina* well before or even while resisting the acquisition of a generalized version of prevoiced glide weakening" (p. 353).

8. Bayley combines 1) strong verbs and copulas other than first person singular and 2) replacives and weak nonsyllabics, citing a small difference in factor values. He justifies these decisions by noting that both verb types in 1) involve a vowel change without affixation of a regular past tense marker (*come—> came*; *is—> was*) and those in 2) involve a change in the final segment (e.g., *send—> sent*; *show—> showed*; *walk—> walked*). The pre- and post-collapse analyses do not differ significantly with respect to goodness of fit (p > .25).

9. Wolfson codes cases like these as ambiguous, as it is unclear whether they are unmarked for third singular or past.

10. The stronger version, termed the 'defective tense hypothesis' emerged in Weist et al. (1984).

11. It is now widely accepted that all varieties of human language are equal (rule governed, systematic and consistent) in linguistic terms. The phenomenon whereby the linguistic varieties of socially subordinate groups are stigmatized as 'dialects' whereas more powerful varieties are elevated to the status of 'languages' is identified by Lippi-Green (1997) as the Principle of Linguistic Subordination. For background on the language-dialect issue, especially in the context of African American English in the US, see Linguistic Society of America (LSA)'s 1997 Resolution on the Ebonics issue, as well as Shuy (1965), Wolfram (1969), and Fasold and Shuy (1970), including updated understandings of how variationists define the linguistic context (e.g., variable rules vs. usage-based effects). Section 3.5 will discuss how the unit of social organization has evolved towards the use of more dynamic categories and concepts (e.g., demographic categories vs. local social networks). Finally, these disciplinary assumptions and methodological traditions will be linked to the research questions addressed by the Durham HE data in the presentation of results in sections 3.5 and 3.6— specifically, the degree to which Durham speech resonates with contemporary accounts of the ethnolect.

12. Kiparsky (1972) attributes the retention of bimorphemic vs. monomorphemic clusters to a difference in functional load, whereby inflectional misse/d/ is preserved over noninflectional mis/t/.ties, the pattern is reversed: their patterns of CCR respond primarily to morphemic status and not as strongly to following phonological environment.
13. Note that chi-square per cell serves a similar purpose to the R^2 statistic discussed in Chapter 5.
14. The standard of 35 or more occurrences per million words—the median for regular past tense forms in Francis and Kučera (1982)—is used as the cut-off point for high vs. low frequency.

References

Adamson, H. D., Fonseca-Greber, B., Kataoka, K., Scardino, V., and S. Takano. 1996. Tense marking in the English of Spanish-speaking adolescents. In Bayley, R., and D. R. Preston, *Second language acquisition and linguistic variation*: 135–176. Philadelphia, PA: John Benjamins.

Adamson, H. D. 2009. *Interlanguage variation in theoretical and pedagogical perspective*. New York: Routledge.

Andersen, R. W. 1989. La adquisición de la morfología verbal. *Lingüística*: 90–142.

Andersen, R. W. 1991. Developmental sequences: The emergence of aspect marking in second language acquisition. In Huebner, T. and C. A. Ferguson (eds.), *Crosscurrents in second language acquisition and linguistic theories*: 305–324. Amsterdam: John Benjamins Publishing Company.

Andersen, R. W., and Y. Shirai. 1994. Discourse motivations for some cognitive acquisition principles. *Studies in Second Language Acquisition 16*: 133–156.

Andersen, R. W., and Y. Shirai. 1996. The primacy of aspect in first and second language acquisition: The pidgin-creole connection. In Ritchie, W. C. and T. K. Bhatia (eds.), *Handbook of second language acquisition*. San Diego, CA: Academic Press.

Antinucci, F., and R. Miller. 1976. How children talk about what happened. *Journal of Child Language 3*: 167–189.

Bardovi-Harlig, K. 1995. A narrative perspective on the development of the tense/aspect system in second language acquisition. *Studies in Second Language Acquisition 17*: 263–291.

Bardovi-Harlig, K., and A. Bergström. 1996. The acquisition of tense and aspect in SLA and FLL: A study of learner narratives in English (SL) and French (FL). *Canadian Modern Language Review 52*: 308–330.

Bayley, R. J. 1991. *Variation theory and second language learning: Linguistic and social constraints on interlanguage tense marking*. Unpublished doctoral dissertation. Stanford University, Stanford, CA.

Bayley, R. J. 1994. Consonant cluster reduction in Tejano English. *Language Variation and Change 6*: 303–326.

Bayley, R. 1999. The primacy of aspect hypothesis revisited: Evidence from language shift. *Southwest Journal of Linguistics: 18:2*.

Bayley, R. J., and J. Langman. 2004. Variation in the group and the individual: Evidence from second language acquisition. *IRAL-International Review of Applied Linguistics in Language Teaching 42*: 303–318.

Benor, S. B. 2010. Ethnolinguistic repertoire: Shifting the analytic focus in language and ethnicity. *Journal of Sociolinguistics 14.2*: 159–183.

Bickerton, D. 1981. *Roots of language*. Ann Arbor, MI: Karoma Publishers.

Bloom, L., K. Lifter, and J. Hafitz. 1980. Semantics of verbs and the development of verb inflection in child language. *Language 56*: 386–412.

Bronckart, J. P., and H. Sinclair. 1973. Time, tense and aspect. *Cognition 2*: 107–130.

Brown, R. 1973. *A first language: The early stages*. Cambridge, MA: Harvard University Press.

Bybee, J. L. 2000a. Lexicalization of sound change and alternating environments. In Broe, M. and J. Pierrehumbert (eds.), *Papers in laboratory phonology 5: Acquisition and the lexicon*: 250–268. New York: Cambridge University Press.

Bybee, J. L. 2000b. The phonology of the lexicon: Evidence from lexical diffusion. In Barlow, M. and S. Kemmer (eds.), *Usage-based models of language*: 65–85. Stanford: CSLI.

Bybee, J. L. 2001. *Phonology and language use*. Cambridge: Cambridge University Press.

Bybee, J. L. 2002. Lexical diffusion in regular sound change. In Restle, D. and D. Zaefferer (eds.), *Sounds and systems: Studies in structure and change*: 59–74. A Festschrift for Theo Vennemann (Trends in Linguistics). Berlin: Mouton de Gruyter.

Bybee, J. L., and O. Dahl. 1989. The creation of tense and aspect systems in the languages of the world. *Studies in Language 13*: 51–103.

Bybee, J. L., R. D. Perkins, and W. Pagliuca. 1994. *The evolution of grammar: Tense, aspect, and modality in the languages of the world*. Chicago: University of Chicago Press.

Callahan, E. E. 2008. *Accommodation without assimilation: Past tense unmarking and peak accent alignment in Hispanic English*. Master's Thesis. North Carolina State University. Retrieved from NCSU Digital Repository <http://repository.lib.ncsu.edu/ir/bitstream/1840.16/2085/1/etd.pdf> on 10/1/2012.

Cazden, C., H. Cancino, Rosansky, E. and J. Schumann. 1975. Second Language Acquisition Sequences in Children, Adolescents and Adults. U.S. Department of Health, Education and Welfare. National Institute of Education Office of Research Grants. Grant No. NE-6-00-3-0014, Project No. 730–744.

Cedergren, H., and D. Sankoff. 1974. Variable rules: Performance as a statistical reflection of competence. *Language 50.2*: 333–355.

Chaudron, C., and K. Parker. 1990. Discourse markedness and structural markedness. *Studies in Second Language Acquisition 12*: 43–64.

Chomsky, N. 1965. *Aspects of the theory of syntax*. Boston: The MIT Press.

Comrie, B. 1976. *Aspect: An introduction to the study of verbal aspect and related problems*. Cambridge: Cambridge University Press.

De Villiers, J. G., and P. A. De Villiers. 1985. The acquisition of English. *The Cross-linguistic Study of Language Acquisition 1*: 27–139.

Dickerson, L. 1975. The learner's interlanguage as a system of variable rules. *Tesol Quarterly 9.4*: 401–407.

Dickerson, W. B. 1976. The psycholinguistic unity of language learning and language change. *Language Learning 26*: 215–231.

Dulay, H. C., and M. K. Burt. 1974. Natural sequences in child second language acquisition. *Language Learning 24*: 37–53.

Ellis, R. 1987. Interlanguage variability in narrative discourse: Style shifting in the use of the past tense. *Studies in Second Language Acquisition 9*: 1–20.

Ellis, R. 1999. Item versus system learning: Explaining free variation. *Applied Linguistics 20.4*: 460–80.

Erker, D., and G. Guy. 2012. The role of lexical frequency in syntactic variability: Variable subject personal pronoun expression in Spanish. *Language 88.3*: 526–557.

Fasold, R. W., and R. W. Shuy (eds). 1970. *Teaching Standard English in the inner city*. Washington, DC: Center for Applied Linguistics.

Fasold, R. 1972. *Tense marking in black English: A linguistic and social analysis*. Arlington, VA: Center for Applied Linguistics.

Fischer, J. L. 1958. Social Influences in the Choice of a Linguistic Variant. *Word 14*: 47–56.

Flashner, V. 1989. Transfer of aspect in the English oral narratives of native Russian speakers. In Dechert, H. W. and M. Raupach (eds.), *Transfer in language production*: 71–97. Norwood, NJ: Able.

Fought, C. 2003. *Chicano English in context*. Basingstoke, UK: Palgrave.

Francis, W. N., and H. Kučera. 1982. *Frequency analysis of English usage: Lexicon and grammar*. Boston: Houghton Mifflin.

Givón, T. 1982. Tense-aspect-modality: The Creole prototype and beyond. In Hopper, P. J. (ed.), *Tense-aspect: Between semantics and pragmatics*: 115–163. Containing the Contributions of a Symposium on Tense and Aspect, Held at UCLA in May 1979. Philadelphia, PA: John Benjamins.

Godfrey D. L. 1980. A Discourse Analysis of Tense in Adult ESL Monologues. In Larsen-Freeman, D. (ed.), *Discourse Analysis in Second Language Research*: 92–110. Rowley: Newbury House

Guy, G. 1980. Variation in the group and the individual: The case of final stop deletion. In Labov, W. (ed.), *Locating language in time and space*: 1–36. New York: Academic Press.

Hopper, P. J. 1979. Aspect and foregrounding in discourse in discourse and syntax. In Givón, T. (ed.), *Syntax and semantics 12: Discourse and Syntax*. New York: Academic Press.

Huebner, T., and D. Bickerton. 1983. *A longitudinal analysis of the acquisition of English*. Ann Arbor, MI: Karoma Publishers.

Johnson, K. 2001. Spoken language variability: Implications for modeling speech perception. In Smits, R., J. Kingston, T. M. Nearey, and R. Zondervan (eds.), *Proceedings of the workshop on Speech Recognition as Pattern Classification (SPRAAC)*. Nijmegen: Max Planck Institute for Psycholinguistics.

Kiparsky, P. 1972. Explanation in phonology. In Peters, S. (ed.), *Goals of linguistic theory*. Englewood Cliffs, NJ: Prentice Hall.

Kumpf, L. 1984. Temporal systems and universality in interlanguage: A case study. In Eckman, F., L. Bell and D. Nelson (eds.), *Universals of second language acquisition*: 132–143. Rowley, MA: Newbury House.

Kurath, H. 1949. *A word geography of the Eastern United States*. Ann Arbor: University of Michigan Press.

Labov, W. 1963. The social motivation of a sound change. *Word 19*: 273–309.

Labov, W. 1969. Contraction, deletion, and inherent variability of the English copula. *Language 45.4*: 715–762.

Labov, W. 1972. *Sociolinguistic patterns*. Philadelphia: University of Pennsylvania Press.

Labov, W. 1989. The exact description of the speech community: Short a in Philadelphia. In R. Fasold and D. Schiffrin (eds.), *Language change and variation*: 1–57. Washington, DC: Georgetown University Press.

Labov, W. 1994. *Principles of linguistic change: Internal factors*. Cambridge, MA: Wiley-Blackwell.

Labov, W. 2010. The diffusion of language from group to group. In Labov, W. (ed.), *Principles of linguistic change* (vol. 3). Oxford: Wiley-Blackwell.

Labov, W., P. Cohen, C. Robins, and J. Lewis. 1968. *A study of the nonstandard English of Negro and Puerto Rican speakers in New York City*. Final Report, Cooperative Research Project No. 3288. United States Office of Education.

Labov, W., and J. Waletzky 1967. Narrative analysis. In Helm, J. (ed.), *Essays on the verbal and visual arts*: 12–44. Seattle: University of Washington Press.

Larsen-Freeman, D. 1980. *Discourse analysis in second language research*. Rowley, MA: Newbury House Publishers.

Lippi-Green, R. 1997. English with an accent. New York: Routledge.

Markee, N. 1994. Toward an ethnomethodological respecification of second language acquisition studies. *Research Methodology in Second Language Acquisition*: 89–116.

Meisel, J. 1987. Reference to past events and actions in the development of natural second language acquisition. In Pfaff, C. W. (ed.), *First and second language acquisition processes*: 206–224. Cambridge, MA: Newbury.

Nordenstam, K. 1979. *Svenskan i Norge*. Gothenberg: University Press.

Phillips, B. S. 1980. Old English *an ~ on*: A new appraisal. *Journal of English Linguistics 14*: 20–23.

Pierrehumbert, J. 2001. Exemplar dynamics: Word frequency, lenition and contrast. In Bybee, J. and P. Hopper (eds.), *Frequency and the emergence of Linguistic structure*: 137–157. Amsterdam: John Benjamins.

Poplack, S. 2001. Variability, frequency and productivity in the irrealis domain of French. In Bybee, J. and P. Hopper (eds.), *Frequency and the emergence of linguistic structure*: 405–428. Amsterdam: Benjamins.

Poplack, S., and S. Tagliamonte. 2001. *African American English in the diaspora*. Cambridge, MA: Wiley-Blackwell.

Preston, D. R. 1989. *Sociolinguistics and second language acquisition*. Oxford: Blackwell.

Preston, D. R. 1996. *Variationist perspectives on second language acquisition: Second language acquisition and linguistic variation*. Oxford: Blackwell.

Preston, D. R., and R. Bayley. 2009. Variationist linguistics and second language acquisition. In Ritchie, W. C. and T. K. Bhatia (eds.), *The new handbook of second language acquisition*: 89–113. London: Emerald Group Publishing Limited.

Reinhart, T. 1984. Principles of gestalt perception in the temporal organization of narrative texts. *Linguistics 22*: 779–810.

Robison, R. E. 1990. The primacy of aspect. *Studies in Second Language Acquisition 12*: 315–330.

Robison, R. E. 1995. The aspect hypothesis revisited: A cross-sectional study of tense and aspect marking in Interlanguage1. *Applied Linguistics 16*: 344–370.

Santa Ana, O. 1991. *Phonetic simplification processes in the English of the barrio: A cross-generational sociolinguistic study of the Chicanos of Los Angeles*. Doctoral dissertation. University of Pennsylvania, Philadelphia, PA.

Santa Ana, O. 1996. Sonority and syllable structure in Chicano English. *Language Variation and Change 8*: 63–89.

Schachter, J. 1986. In search of systematicity in interlanguage production. Studies in Second Language Acquisition 8: 119–33.

Schecter, S. R., and R. Bayley. 2002. *Language as cultural practice: Mexicanos en el norte*. Mahwah, NJ: Lawrence Erlbaum.

Selinker, L. 1972. *Interlanguage. International Review of Applied Linguistics 10*: 209–231.

Shirai, Y., and R. W. Andersen. 1995. The acquisition of tense-aspect morphology: A prototype account. *Language 71.4*: 743–762.

Shirai, Y., and A. Kurono. 1998. The acquisition of tense-aspect marking in Japanese as a second language. *Language Learning 48*: 279–44.

Shuy, R. W. (ed). 1965. *Social dialects and language learning*. Champaign, Ill.: National Council of Teachers of English.

Shuy, R. W. 2003. A brief history of American sociolinguistics: 1949–1989. In C. Paulston and G. R. Tucker (eds.), *Sociolinguistics: The essential readings*. Malden, MA: Blackwell.

Slobin, D. I. 1985. Crosslinguistic evidence for the language-making capacity. *The Crosslinguistic Study of Language Acquisition 2*: 1157–1256.

Stephany, U. 1981. Verbal grammar in modern Greek early child language. In Dale, P. S. and D. Ingram (eds.), *Child language: An international perspective*: 45–57. Baltimore: University Park Press.

Tarone, E. 1979. Interlanguage as chameleon. *Language Learning 29*: 181–191.

Tarone, E. 1981. Some thoughts on the notion of communication strategy. *Tesol Quarterly 15*: 285–295.

Tarone, E. 1990. On variation interlanguage: A response to Gregg. *Applied Linguistics 11*: 392–400.

Trudgill, P. 1986. *Dialects in contact*. Oxford: Basil Blackwell.

Vendler, Z. 1967. *Linguistics in philosophy. Ithaca*: Cornell University Press.

Véronique, D. 1987. Reference to past events and actions in narratives in L2: Insights from north African learners' French. In Pfaff, C. W. (ed.), *First and second language acquisition processes*: 252–272. Rowley, MA: Newbury House.

Wang, W. S.-Y., and C.-C. Cheng. 1977. Implementation of phonological change: The Shûangfêng Chinese case. In W. S.-Y. Wang (ed.), *The lexicon in phonological change*. The Hague: Mouton.

Weinreich, U., W. Labov, and M. Herzog. 1968. Empirical foundations for a theory of language change. In Lehmann, W. P. and Y. Malkeil (eds.), *Directions for historical linguistics: A symposium*: 95–188. Austin: University of Texas Press.

Weist, R. M., H. Wyscocka, K. Witkowska-Stadnik, E. Buczowka, and E. Konieczna. 1984. The defective tense hypothesis: On the emergence of tense and aspect in child Polish. *Journal of Child Language 11*: 347–374.

Wolfram, W. 1969. *A linguistic description of detroit Negro speech*. Washington, DC: Center for Applied Linguistics.

Wolfram, W. 1974. *A sociolinguistic study of assimilation: Puerto Rican English in New York City*. Washington, DC: Center for Applied Linguistics.

Wolfram, W. 1978. Contrastive linguistics and social lectology. *Language Learning 28*: 1–28.

Wolfram, W., R. Childs, and B. Torbert. 2000. Tracing English dialect history through consonant cluster reduction: Comparative evidence from isolated dialects. *Journal of Southern Linguistics 24*: 17–40.

Wolfram, W., and D. Christian. 1976. *Appalachian speech*. Arlington, VA: Center for Applied Linguistics.

Wolfram, W., and R. W. Fasold. 1974. *The study of social dialects in the United States*. Englewood Cliffs: Prentice Hall.

Wolfram, W., and D. Hatfield. 1984. *Tense marking in second language learning: Patterns of spoken and written English in a Vietnamese community*. Washington, DC: Center for Applied Linguistics.

Wolfson, N. 1982. On tense alternation and the need for analysis of native speaker usage in second language acquisition. *Language Learning 32*: 53–68.

Young, R. 1996. Form-function relations in articles in English interlanguage. In Bayley, R., and D. R. Preston (eds.), *Second language acquisition and linguistic variation*: 135–176. Philadelphia, PA: John Benjamins.

Young, R. 1999. Sociolinguistic approaches to SLA. *Annual Review of Applied Linguistics 19*: 105–132.

3   The Speech Community

Ethnolect Formation, Development
and Contexts of Use

EC [Interviewer/INT]:	Are there gangs here—a lot of gangs?
Silvia:	Uh-huh.
Elizabeth:	Yeah.
EC:	Really? What kind? What are the, like, do you know—
Silvia:	Yesterday, it was, um, a sixth-grade Traditional[1] had a gun.
EC:	In the school?
Silvia:	In the school.
EC:	That's really scary.
Silvia:	Mm-hm.
EC:	What happened? Tell me what happened.
Silvia:	He, um, he was pushing the, um, police. He was like, um, "Get off of me!" and all that. And he was pushing and the-
Elizabeth:	He push her over the wall. It was a, um, woman.
INT 2:	It was a policewoman?
Elizabeth:	Yeah. She work here. And then the other one, a man, a man police came, and then—they get him with the principals, there are three [principals].
INT 2:	Did you know that kid?
Elizabeth:	Um, no.
Silvia:	Uh-uh.
Elizabeth:	Well, he just talk me one time. Like, my first time, I get here, and I was like "Where am I?" I get lost, 'cause I came to this wall, and not other one. And then he help me, and then I went to my class.
EC:	Wow! So what happened when they found the gun? Did they-
Silvia:	He got suspended for the rest of the year.
[SEVEN MINUTES PASS]	

INT 2:	Do you- when something like that happens, a fight, or somebody has a gun, or the cutting—do your teachers try to talk to get the class to talk about it, and talk about how it made you feel?
Silvia:	Mm-hmm.
Elizabeth:	Yeah.
EC:	What do people say? Are they scared, or sad, or angry—how do they feel?
Elizabeth:	The teachers? Or the one who got-
EC:	Both people. I mean, like the other kids in the class-
Elizabeth:	Yeah.
Silvia:	Um, the boy got cut—um, everybody was sad. 'Cause he's our friend. Everybody was sad. But I was crying, and—they were just sad. And I was crying [laughs].
INT 2:	Yeah, sometimes—you were probably crying because you were sad and 'cause you were scared.
Silvia:	Mm-hm.
Elizabeth:	Yeah.
INT 2:	'Cause when something like that happens, you think, "Oh, it could have just been me walking down the hall. . . ."
Silvia:	Mm-hm.
Elizabeth:	But, she was just trying to cut him. Not everyb- not someone else.
INT 2:	She wanted to cut him.
Elizabeth:	Just him.
Elizabeth:	Yeah, and when we saw him, he was in the trash can, just bleeding.
EC:	So wait—did you find him?
Elizabeth:	Yeah. He was in the classroom. And the teachers were out at the hall. And then we called them.
Silvia:	And then he went to the classroom, and he was at the trash can, with tissues—trying to clean himself. And the teacher saw him, and they took him to to the office. And they call their parents, and they called the parents of the girl cut them. And—that's what happened.
EC:	Wow . . . what did your parents say about it?
Silvia:	Mm, like, that she was crazy or—mm-hm.
Elizabeth:	Yeah.

3.0   Welcome to Durham: Elizabeth and Silvia

Elizabeth and Silvia are both 12-years old and in the 7th grade. They have both been in the US for three years and are both from Mexico: Elizabeth from the state of Oaxaca and Silvia from *D.F.*, [Districto Federal], Mexico City. Silvia's favorite class is math and Elizabeth's is social studies, where they are learning about Africa. One of their favorite teachers is Miss G-, because she is *buena gente*: she helps them with their work when they need it and also listens to them talk about their problems. Most of their best friends are Hispanic, with whom they speak English about half the time and Spanish half the time. Elizabeth also has a close friend, Lindsay, who is white and speaks only English. Both girls speak mostly Spanish with their parents—though Silvia says her mom understands little things in English, like "I'm hungry," "Can I go outside?" or "I love you." Elizabeth says she likes speaking English so she can learn more and Spanish "so she doesn't forget it." Both girls list their favorite music as bach-ata, merengue and reggaeton (which Silvia describes as " R&B")—but both girls say they don't like rap. Elizabeth wants to visit Miami and Silvia wants to visit New York, because it's "bigger, with more people walking around." They both like *mole* and *tamales*. Both girls giggle uncontrollably when the interviewer's phone rings near the end of the interview, playing a Johnny Cash ringtone, "Ring of Fire." Silvia's dad is in Mexico and her mom cleans offices. Elizabeth's dad is a mechanic and her mother works in the fast food restaurant Chick-Fil-A, which is based in the US south. When asked what they want to be when they grow up, both girls say they want to be doctors.

In this chapter, I will talk about Durham, NC as a *place*—a place at the intersection of Englishes and Spanishes (and indigenous L1s like Otomí, Nahuatl and Maya), of regions (the US south vs. the US urban northeast and Chicano southwest) and of neighborhoods—in order to provide a broader social context for the study.

3.1   Site, Speakers and Methods

In this section, I will discuss the site where the data for this study was col-lected, the general characteristics of the speakers involved, and methods used for collecting the data. I will then discuss in detail the conventions I used and decisions I made in transcribing and coding. Finally, I will provide examples of conversational excerpts with individual speakers in order to illustrate how this coding took place in practice.

3.1.1   *Durham Speech Community: Demographics and Trends*

In the past few decades, North Carolina has experienced a population boom of Spanish-speaking residents that is emblematic of the southeast-ern US in general. Between 2000 and 2010, more than half the increase in population in the US as a whole was due to the growth in Hispanic or Latino origin respondents; during this period, the Hispanic population grew by 43% nationwide and by more than 3 million people, four times the growth of the total US population. The group of US residents who identified a Hispanic or Latino origin[2] has grown fastest in the South, which experienced a 57% growth as a region overall from 2000 to 2010 (vs. 49% in the Midwest, and only 34% and 33% respectively in the West and Northeast). In fact, in the two-decade span from 1990 to 2000 and then from 2000 to 2010, growth across the South stayed in the triple digits, far outpacing traditional Hispanic strongholds including California, New York and Texas (Figure 3.1).

As the bottom half of Figure 3.1 shows, North Carolina led the South overall in Hispanic population growth from 1990 to 2010 (it had highest growth rate in the nation from 1990 to 2000 and the sixth-highest rate from 2000 to 2010). This growth has been constituted mostly through in-migration from speakers of Mexican (60.9% as of 2010) and Central American origin, including the three most populous Central American origin groups, made up of Salvadoran (4.7%), Honduran (3.9%) and Guatemalan (2.5%) residents. This in-migration to 'new destinations' (Flippen and Parrado 2012) like Durham and Atlanta, GA (as well as other places in the Southeast and Midwest)—which are both more decentralized than traditional, pre-war urban cities and also unused to large, rapid immigration inflows—is newer than traditional immigration to US urban centers like New York City and Miami, Florida.

Durham, NC is a triethnic, medium-sized city in the heavily developed Research Triangle Park region of the North Carolina Piedmont. After the Civil War, Durham's growth was propelled by the success of the city's tobacco mills in the early 1900s, facilities that processed the popular 'Brightleaf' tobacco. The late 1950s heralded the formation of the special tax district Research Triangle Park (RTP) between Durham and Raleigh, NC, which drew research and development firms to the area from the north. During waves of suburbanization during the 1960s and 1970s, Durham's population moved outward to meet new large-scale subdivisions, apartment complexes, malls and office parks. During this period, in an attempt to revitalize Durham's downtown and clear the area for the construction of the Durham Freeway (which runs between Durham, RTP, and Raleigh), large sections of Durham's historically Black neighborhoods were demolished, including Hayti, an independent Black community formed after the Civil War; "Black Wall Street," which bordered Hayti and housed the nation's largest Black-owned insurance company, North Carolina Mutual Life Insurance; and the historically Black university, North Carolina Central, which joined the state's public university system in 1972. A collection of historic neighborhoods remains preserved in and

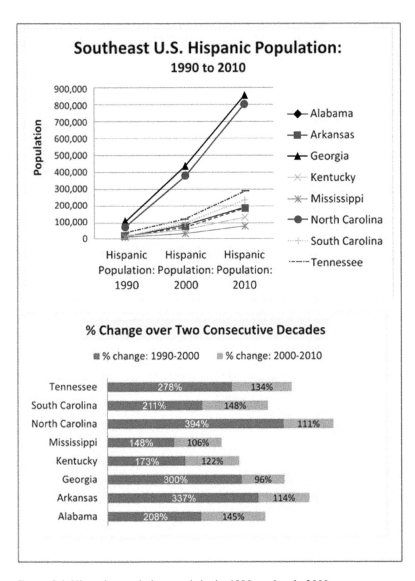

Figure 3.1 Hispanic population trends in the 1990s and early 2000s

around Durham downtown and Duke University, located less than a mile to the west. Like other metro regions in the Southeast, Durham's level of racial segregation is lower than larger urban areas in the northern and midwestern US; its 2010 Black–white index of dissimilarity of 48.1 (the percentage of a city's population that would have to move to achieve equal distribution) falls significantly below cities like metro New York (78.0), Detroit (75.3), Pittsburgh, PA (65.8) and Baltimore (64.4) (see www.censusscope.org/segregation.html). Interestingly, Flippen and Parrado (2012) point out that the 2000 Hispanic-white index of dissimilarity in Durham (64.0) was actually higher than that of Blacks. A 2014 NBC News story reports that the establishment of one of the city's largest Hispanic supermarkets, La Superior, was due to the owner only being able to buy the property with grants and a 2001 loan from Mechanics & Farmer's Bank, a historically Black-owned institution located on "Black Wall Street." Conservative estimates by the UNC Latino Migration Project— which assume immigration rates will actually fall—predict that by 2020 one in three children born in Durham will be of Hispanic/Latino origin.

Though it has tapered off since the Great Recession, Hispanic population growth still accounts for more than half of total US population growth between 2000 and 2014, with North Carolina in the top 5 states in the US for the share of Latinos who are foreign born, all of them in the US south (Stepler and Lopez 2016). As of 2002, the US Census Bureau established that Hispanics outnumber African Americans as the largest minority group in the country (Ramirez and Patricia de la Cruz 2002). As we approach becoming a "majority-minority" country around the tipping point date 2044 (Colby and Ortman 2014), the social landscape will be a very different one.

Early (pre-1990) immigration to Durham was centered around agriculture (e.g., tobacco, Christmas trees, greenhouse, cucumbers) and the construction boom associated with the high-tech industry. As of 2004, the year before this study, 41.4% of Hispanics in North Carolina were US citizens by birth and 45% were living in the state without documentation (Kasarda and Johnson 2006); this same year, Durham was number 5 in the state for North Carolina counties with the largest public school Hispanic enrollment (NC State Board of Education and NC Department of Public Instruction 2005).

In addition to Hispanics and European Americans, African Americans make up a sizeable portion of Durham's population and are in the majority of students attending the city's public schools. Figure 3.2 shows the overall population of Durham using self-report figures from the 2010 Census.

Like the city of Durham itself, the three schools chosen for this project (funded under National Science Foundation Grants BCS-0213941 and BCS-0542139) are characterized by large African American student populations. The schools were chosen in consultation with Durham Public Schools

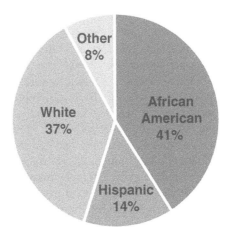

Figure 3.2 Race for Durham (city), NC (%)

K-12 English as a Second Language (ESL) Services staff, including director Sashi Rayasam, a former professional contact of the author, and principal investigator Walt Wolfram.

3.2   Ethnographic Evidence

I had personal experience working in the school system and living in the community represented by the three study sites. During 2002 to 2003, I taught Spanish and French (as foreign languages) at Hillside High School, a historically Black high school and social institution in Durham's African American community (Frazier 1925). Rogers-Herr, one of schools in this study, 'feeds into' Hillside High according to Durham Public School's districting plan, so many of the students I taught had attended middle school there. In addition, I was an ESL teacher at the second study site, Chewning Middle, during the summer of 2003; all my 15 or so students that summer were L1 Spanish speakers from various parts of Latin America. During the 2003–2004 and 2004–2005 school years, I moved to a position teaching ESL in Granville County Schools, a rural county just north of the Durham city limits (one of the study sites, Chewning Middle, is located less than a mile from the Granville County line). Finally, I was a resident of Durham's Old West Durham/Ninth Street neighborhood during the period from 2001 to 2005. E.K. Powe, the one elementary school in the study, is located on the four-block Ninth Street business and residential corridor in Durham between Hillsborough Road and West Club Boulevard.

The three schools have different characters, part of which is formed by their distinct demographic and geographic profiles (Figure 3.3).

E.K. Powe Elementary has the highest Hispanic population (28%) and draws from five economically diverse, densely populated urban neighborhoods near downtown Durham (Watts-Hillandale, Crest Street, Walltown, Old West Durham and the West End). Spanish-speaking parents often walk their children to school, which is located on one whole city block, and Spanish-speaking families use the school's playing fields many afternoons for pick-up soccer games. During the time I lived and did fieldwork near the school, its sign outside often had its weekly welcome posted in both English and Spanish.

By contrast, Chewning Middle is located in a rural setting with over 20 acres of buildings and grounds. The school is in a much less densely populated area in more remote northeast Durham, accessed most easily via Interstate I-85, and is located about a mile from both the Eno River and

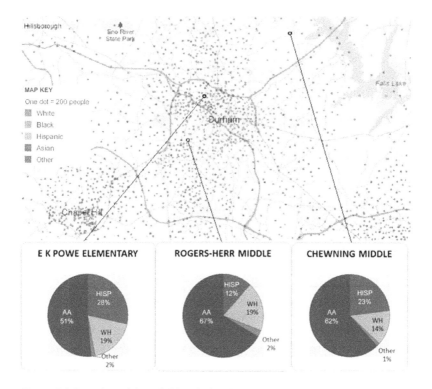

Figure 3.3 Location of three fieldwork sites in Durham, NC

Falls Lake, which extends into adjacent Wake and Granville County (NC). The third school, Rogers-Herr, has the lowest Hispanic population (12%) and is somewhere 'between' E.K. Powe and Chewning demographically. It is located outside of Durham's urban core in a somewhat more suburban setting that is less densely populated than the center of Durham but more populated than the rural setting of Chewning. Academically, Chewning was the lowest-performing school during the 2006–2007 academic year, with less than 50% of students overall performing at grade level on end-of-year standardized tests (NC Department of Public Instruction 2005). E.K. Powe had between 50% and 60% of students performing at grade level and Rogers-Herr had the highest-performing students, with 60–80% of students performing at grade level.

3.3   Speakers

Speakers were drawn from the three schools in Durham (one elementary school and two middle schools) and ranged in age from 9 to 14 (grades 4 through 8). Speakers participated in sociolinguistic interviews performed by bilingual graduate student fieldworkers, mostly English (sociolinguistics) master's degree students associated with North Carolina Language and Life Project (NCLLP) at North Carolina State University. These interviews were conducted during late 2006 and early 2007, and are currently archived online in the Sociolinguistic Archive and Analysis Project database (SLAAP) (Kendall 2007). In most cases, the Spanish and English interviews were conducted on different occasions by different interviewers. Speakers, especially in Durham, were interviewed in dyads whenever possible to increase comfort level. Topics in both the English and Spanish interviews included the typical everyday interests of US elementary and middle school students: school events, movies, recreational activities, video games and dating. Interviews at E.K. Powe took place in the classroom of the school's ESL teacher. Middle school interviews were usually held in whatever empty classrooms were available during the school day, though a few interviews took place in an empty cafeteria or the school media center. Either immediately before or after the conversational interview, fieldworkers briefly collected survey data that listed basic demographic and social information for the speaker, including birthplace, LOR, family composition, best friends, music tastes, language use patterns (who spoke which language(s) to whom in the family) and language in which the child learned to read.

In addition to English and Spanish sociolinguistic interviews, which typically lasted around 45 minutes and were conducted during the school day, structured education data were collected from some students. Though these measures were not used directly in this analysis, they were occasionally used to verify the child's reported literacy in English and/or Spanish. The academic language protocols included a reading/translation task in which children read one to three short picture book stories in English, then spontaneously translated the stories orally to Spanish, followed by standardized testing in English and Spanish, using the Woodcock-Johnson (WJ-III) tests of achievement (Schrank et al. 2005).

3.4 Moving into the Community

In the same way that quantitative methodologies (and their underlying assumptions) have evolved over the lifetime of variationist sociolinguistics, the unit of social organization has changed from the static demographic categories discussed in section 4.2 (region, ethnicity, class, even gang affiliation) to integrate more dynamic, local and participant-driven social categories and the social meanings these participants index in discourse (Eckert 2000). This widening lens can also capture those intersections that spell out important generalities about language variation and change in social space. For example, by using a "friend of a friend" technique to access social networks, Milroy and Milroy (1978) first established how dense, multiplex ties constrained phonological variation in three urban, working-class neighborhoods in Belfast, Northern Ireland. Later research (Milroy and Milroy 1993; Docherty et al. 1997) was then able to piece together a workable explanation for gendered use of more standard norms in terms of the more precise formalizations spelled out by the network dynamics of an actual community. Specifically, Milroy (1999) gives an explicit account of how male peer networks can constrain speech by preserving conservative, local norms whereas women's broader network ties facilitate their mobility as innovators.

A subsequent strand of research using the Community of Practice (CofP) framework (Eckert and McConnell-Ginet 1992) showed how local categories actually *constitute* traditional census' categories like race or gender (Fought 1997) as identities in locally determined ways. These community-specific constructs turn out to explain variation in more useful terms than local or global characterizations alone—as in the construction of a 'jock' vs. 'burnout' (Eckert 1989), 'nerd girl' (Bucholtz 1999) or *Norteña/Sureña* identity (Mendoza-Denton 1997).

These network and CofP studies illustrate how intersections are often the key to unlocking lower-level generalities about language variation and change. Both linguistic and social structure are coded at multiple levels of redundancy, and it has often been at the intersections of traditional and novel categories—and the conversations between them—that we find revealing patterns that drive the discipline forward to a level of greater coherence. Here, the intersections of new and old categories—network structure with gender, adolescent peer structure with class, or morphemic status and phonological environment—provide important opportunities to make higher-order generalizations about how variation and change function in general.

3.5   Ethnolects

Since the earliest studies of variationist sociolinguistics, researchers have referred broadly to ethnic dialects or varieties, including African American (Vernacular) English (e.g., Labov 1972; Fasold 1972; Baugh 1983; Green 2002) and Chicano English (Fought 2006; Mendoza-Denton 2008). Most, if not all, of these authors have qualified their accounts by noting that not all members of an ethnic group speak the (one) ethnic variety under consideration; it is now established, for example, that AAE is stratified by class (Wolfram and Fasold 1974; Rickford 1999; Weldon 2004) and is neither structurally nor regionally homogenous (Wolfram 2007).

In studies of L2 English populations, the general term *ethnolect* (Clyne 2000; Wolck 2002) has been used to describe the English of ethnic immigrants, which may be marked by a L1 substrate influence as speakers shift from monolingualism to bilingualism. Just as early variationist studies, to varying degrees, treated ethnically associated dialects are socially and structurally homogenous, some early ethnolect accounts were written in terms of social uniformity. Recent research has challenged the static ethnolectal account. For example, research on phonological variation in multiethnic New York City (Becker and Coggshall 2009; Becker 2014), in northern California (Eckert 2008) and on Jewish American English in the US (Benor 2010) has contributed to the theme that ethnicity can be thought of as a more dynamic entity than that which has sometimes been assumed (e.g., of ethnic varieties of Chicano or African American English as such). One influential account has been that of an *ethnolinguistic repertoire* (Benor 2010), which is defined as "a fluid set of linguistic resources that members of an ethnic group may use variably as they index their ethnic identities" (160). The repertoire model resists treating ethnic varieties as a separate linguistic entities (Fought 2003) and instead sees variable structures as more or less regionally and ethnically distinct resources that speakers may map on to a diverse set of values, orientations, identities, aspirations, alignments and day-to-day needs.

For example, in an ethnographic study of preadolescent speech in two schools in northern California (the working-class, largely Chicano and Asian 'Steps' Elementary vs. the largely Anglo, middle-class 'Fields Elementary' only 10 miles away), Eckert (2008) shows how features like prenasal /ae/ (raised before nasals in Anglo varieties and 'lowered'—or simply unraised—in Chicano varieties of English) become a 'second order index' used for purposes beyond marking ethnicity. Instead, the indexing of sociolinguistic variables initiates speakers into crowd membership and a sense of 'coolness' associated with a peer-based social order centered around the heterosexual marketplace. Similarly, Slomanson and Newman (2004) show how affiliation with a peer group culture (including hip-hoppers, skaters, geeks, and nonparticipants in high school peer cultures) correlates with lateral (l) variation[3] in New York Latino English (NYLE). Moving globally, Sharma (2011) uses the repertoire approach to analyze both British- and Punjabi-derived phonological traits, including retroflexion of /t/[4] in second-generation British Asians; she finds a reversal of gender roles has occurred over time from Asian, lower-middle class to more typical British lower-middle/working-class orientation.

These approaches that break down barriers between bounded, uniform ethnic 'varieties' of English are useful in at least some ways for considering the data in the Durham study: they help establish the playing field as a "landscape in which ethnicity plays a prominent but not determining role" (Eckert 2008: 41) and where variable features are not necessarily understood only in terms of Anglo/white English, but in terms of a shared community use. As we will see in later chapters, features that may be thought of as distinctively African American, including habitual *be* and double marking of possessives (*mines*), occur across the board in Durham HE by speakers of all ages and both genders, as well as by gang-affiliated and non-gang-affiliated students (Table 4.3 in Chapter 4 shows a brief selection of identifiably AAE features).

One key thread in most accounts of ethnolinguistic repertoire involves the central role of speaker agency, which is operationalized in different ways—including signaling aspects of social identity in particular settings (Doran 2004: 94), using variants 'strategically,' (Hoffman and Walker 2010), signaling bicultural identity via (oppositional) stances (Damari 2010) —to negotiate identities through language and to (optionally) construct ethnicity itself (Slomanson and Newman 2004: 214–215). Notably, some authors allow both automatic and nonautomatic processes to constitute ethnolinguistic repertoire, including Benor (2010), who sees speakers "using linguistic variation—consciously or subconsciously—to align themselves with some people and distinguish themselves from others" (p. 160), and Eckert, who characterizes repertoires as "a set of resources that speakers deploy both intentionally and automatically in their day-to-day practice" (Eckert 2008: 26). Still, much of the work on ethnolinguistic repertoire uses a decidedly Second or Third Wave theoretical lens (Eckert 2008), in which linguistic variation is a reflection of social identities or, in the more dynamic view, a stylistic practice in which speakers (from all communities) can appropriate sociolinguistic variables to index contextually determined, idiosyncratic stances in moment-by-moment interactions. The indexical appropriation involves, for example, the use of individual Mandarin variables including nonmainland 'full tone' as the speech style used by young managers in Beijing's wealthy elite 'yuppies' (Zhang 2005).

Under this view, the Durham data are more in line with Fought (2006), who, in a study of Chicano English in Los Angeles, describes the ethnolect as a "pool of resources from which members of a speech community draw the linguistic tools they need" (p. 21).

The data in this study show that in terms of CCR, at least, patterns are accessible to a broad range of Durham speakers, regardless of ethnicity or even language proficiency. In this sense, the Durham data demonstrate how a 'pool of resources' might be more usefully considered in terms of the local lexicon itself. As the Durham speakers acquire a particular local variety of English (e.g., that of African American (AA) peers), they must pay attention to the combinations of words around them (in other words, usage-based effects in the input, which we will return to in Chapter 4). As Durham language learners keep track of how these effects intersect (for example, the intersection of phonological environment and morphemic status), then they learn speech norms in this community. In this sense, the words around them—their local, everyday linguistic experience—is absolutely critical to becoming a member of the Durham speech community as a 'repertoire' that is accessible to all speakers regardless of ethnicity. In fact, as we will see in Chapter 4, both the African American and Hispanic speakers in this study chose the same combinations of words (e.g., in terms of phonological and morphemic status) to use in everyday discourse—patterns that bring to life variable effects.

The link here between local language/dialect acquisition and contemporary 'ethnolect' models is between language use (i.e., anyone can access sound changes in progress regardless of ethnicity) and usage. The usage-based account (e.g., in terms of underlying interaction phonological/morphological interactions like more bimorphemes before vowels) still provides for a flexible, fluid baseline of 'resources' in terms of patterns of use. In this sense, HE speakers are not necessarily 'accommodating' or 'aligning' with their African American peers or creating unique 'stances' as such—they're just sharing language/diffusing norms and doing so regardless of ethnicity.

I will ultimately make the case in Chapter 4 that Durham speakers' shared experience with a common set of words (and combinations of words) that they hear and use to talk about their daily lives and shared environment (a corpus or lexicon) may outline the most useful kind of 'speech community' for the results in this study. Here, language learners in Durham help distill some of the most frequent (and immediately useful) components of this shared toolkit, patterns which are then not discarded by native speakers, just supplemented and amplified. In all, the Durham data help establish that 'categories' like ethnicity (Hispanic vs. African American) and proficiency (native vs. nonnative)—and, in turn, static ethnolects—are fairly leaky concepts, sociolinguistically speaking.

In this sense, the Durham data demonstrate how a 'pool of resources' might be more usefully considered in terms of the local lexicon itself. As the Durham speakers acquire a particular local variety of English (e.g., that of African American peers), they must pay attention to the combinations of words around them (in other words, usage-based effects in the input, which we will return to in Chapter 4). As Durham language learners keep track of how these effects intersect (for example, the intersection of phonological environment and morphemic status), then they learn speech norms in this community. In this sense, the words around them—their local, everyday linguistic experience—is absolutely critical to becoming a member of the Durham speech community as a 'repertoire' that is accessible to all speakers regardless of ethnicity. In fact, as we will see in Chapter 4, both the African American and Hispanic speakers in this study chose the same combinations of words (e.g., in terms of phonological and morphemic status) to use in everyday discourse—patterns that bring to life variable effects.

3.6   Conclusions

As a contradiction-ridden whole, the Durham speakers demonstrate a fundamental principle of the 'speech community' construct that remains elusive even four decades later: speakers at once share many norms, but at the same time show very distinct patterns across class membership categories. While the assertion noted in this chapter—no two speakers, regardless of how many types of group membership they share, ever speak exactly the same way—it is simultaneously true that, to accomplish social life through language, speakers must use and evaluate forms in recognizably similar ways:

> Every concrete utterance of a speaking subject serves as a point where centrifugal as well as centripetal forces are brought to bear. The processes of centralization and decentralization, of unification and disunification, intersect in the utterance; the utterance not only answers the requirements of its own language as an individualized embodiment of a speech act, but it answers the requirements of heteroglossia as well; it is in fact an active participant in such speech diversity. . . . Such is the fleeting language of a day, of an epoch, a social group, a genre, a school

and so forth. It is possible to give a concrete and detailed analysis of any utterance, once having exposed it as a contradiction-ridden, tension-filled unity of two embattled tendencies in the life of language.

(Bahktin 1981: 272)

It is in this context that researchers must recognize the Herculean task of Second Language Acquisition—a process during which speakers must, as all of us do, speak both the same and differently at the same time. While no two utterances a language learner hears are ever exactly alike, he must work out which differences are special and in what way. This requires processing multiple semiotic systems, establishing connections, uncovering regularities, then assigning those regularities reliable (and, indeed, socially useful) meanings. Especially outside the context of formal instruction (where content meanings and rules may be specified explicitly), the language learner must accomplish a tandem task of meaning-making every time she produces an utterance: she must say *what* she wants to say while saying it the *way* she wants to say it. Even more dauntingly, these two tasks must be accomplished simultaneously—with very few do-overs.

Notes

1. In Silvia's and Elizabeth's school, students can choose to attend according to either a 'traditional' calendar (students attend school August through June, with an extended summer vacation) or a 'year-round' calendar (students attend for 45 days, then have a 3-week 'intersession' break).
2. The US Census methodology for determining Hispanic origin has also undergone a transformation in the last half century. Prior to the 1970 Census, the Bureau's Hispanic 'identifiers' consisted of responses to questions that asked about place of birth, Spanish mother tongue and Spanish surname. The origin self-report question was introduced in 1970 and classifies a respondent as Hispanic or Latino if she responds that she is "a person of Cuban, Mexican, Puerto Rican, South or Central American, or other Spanish culture or origin regardless of race." Here, the concepts of ethnicity and race are separate and distinct concepts, with Hispanic origin defined as "the heritage, nationality group, lineage, or country of birth of the person or the person's parents or ancestors before their arrival in the United States." Thus, residents of Hispanic origin may be of any race.
3. L1 Spanish varieties of English in the US may variably use the substrate feature 'light' [l]. Light/Spanish [l] is produced with a neutral tongue body position while 'dark' [ɫ], the variant used in mainstream American English codas, is produced with tongue body raised to the position for back vowels (Slomanson and Newman 2004). Perceptually speaking, I observed various degrees of (coda) light [l] in the Durham NCHE data.
4. Punjabi distinguishes between retroflex and dental stops, while British English contrasts only voiceless and voiced alveolar stops /t/ and /d/; in many varieties of Indian English, the alveolar stops are replaced by retroflex [ʈ] and [ɖ] (Bhatia 1993). The other variables in Sharma (2011) are the FACE and GOAT vowel as well as coda /l/.

References

Bahktin, M. M. 1981. In Holquist, M. (ed.) and Emerson, C. and M. Holquist (transl.), *The dialogic imagination: Four essays by M.M. Bahktin.* Austin, TX: University of Texas Press.

Baugh, J. 1983. *Black street speech: Its history, structure and survival.* Austin, TX: University of Texas Press.

Becker, K. 2014. Forthcoming: Ethnolect, dialect, and linguistic repertoire in New York City. In Yaeger-Dror, M. and Hall-Lew (eds.), *New perspectives on the concept of the ethnolect.*

Becker, K., and E. L. Coggshall. 2009. The sociolinguistics of ethnicity in New York City. *Language and Linguistic Compass 3.3*: 751–766.

Benor, S. B. 2010. Ethnolinguistic repertoire: Shifting the analytic focus in language and ethnicity. *Journal of Sociolinguistics 14.2*: 159–183.

Bucholtz, M. 1999. 'Why be normal?': Language and identity practices in a community of nerd girls. *Language in Society 28.2*: 203–223.

Clyne, M. 2000. Lingua franca and ethnolects. *Sociolinguistica 14*: 83–89.

Colby, S. L., and J. M. Ortman. 2014. *Projections of the size and composition of the U.S. population: 2014 to 2060.* Current Population Reports, P25–1143. U.S. Census Bureau, Washington, DC.

Damari, R. R. 2010. A phonetic analysis of stancetaking by a binational couple. Paper presented at Sociolinguistics Symposium 18, Southampton, UK.

Docherty, G. P., J. Foulkes, J. Milroy, L. Milroy, and D. Walshaw. 1997. Descriptive adequacy in phonology: A variationist perspective. *Journal of Linguistics 33*: 1–36.

Doran, M. 2004. Negotiating between 'Bourge' and 'Racaille': Verlan as youth identity practice in Suburban Paris. In Pavlenko, A. and A. Blackledge (eds.), *Negotiation of identities in multilingual contexts.* Clevedon: Multilingual Matters, 93–124.

Eckert, P. 1989. *Jocks and Burnouts.* New York: Teachers College Press.

Eckert, P. 2000. *Language variation as social practice.* Oxford: Basil Blackwell.

Eckert, P. 2008. Where do ethnolects stop? *International Journal of Bilingualism 12.1–2*: 25–42.

Eckert, P., and S. McConnell-Ginet. 1992. Think practically and look locally: Language and gender as community-based practice. *Language in Society 28*: 185–201.

Fasold, R. 1972. *Tense marking in black English: A linguistic and social analysis.* Arlington, VA: Center for Applied Linguistics.

Flippen, C. A., and E. A. Parrado. 2012. Forging ispanic communities in new destinations: A case study of Durham, North Carolina. *City & Community 11.1*: 1–30.

Fought, C. 1997. A majority sound change in a minority community: /u/-fronting in Chicano English. *Journal of Sociolinguistics 3.1*: 5–23.

Fought, C. 2003. *Chicano English in context.* Basingstoke, UK: Palgrave.

Fought, C. 2006. *Language and ethnicity.* Cambridge: Cambridge University Press.

Frazier, E. F. 1925. Durham, capital of the black middle class. In Locke A. (ed.), *The New Negro: Voice of the harlem renaissance*: 333. New York: Albert & Charles Boni.

Green, L. 2002. *African American English: A linguistic introduction.* Cambridge: Cambridge University Press.

Hoffman, M., and J. Walker. 2010. Ethnolects and the city: Ethnic orientation and linguistic variation in Toronto English. *Language Variation and Change 22*: 37–67.

Kendall, T. 2007. The North Carolina sociolinguistic archive and analysis project: Empowering the sociolinguistic archive. *Penn Working Papers in Linguistics 13.2*: 15–26. Philadelphia: University of Pennsylvania.

Labov, W. 1972. *Sociolinguistic patterns*. Philadelphia: University of Pennsylvania Press.

Mendoza-Denton, N. 1997. *Chicana/Mexicana identity and linguistic variation: An ethnographic and sociolinguistic study of gang affiliation in an urban high school.* Ph.D. dissertation. Stanford University.

Mendoza-Denton, N. 2008. *Homegirls: Language and cultural practice among Latina youth gangs*. Oxford, UK: Blackwell.

Milroy, L. 1999. Women as innovators and norm-creators: The sociolinguistics of dialect leveling in a northern English city. In Wertheim, S., A. C. Bailey and M. Corston-Oliver (eds.), *Engendering Communication*, Proceedings of the Fifth Berkeley Women and Language Conference: 361–376.

Milroy, J., and L. Milroy. 1978. Belfast: Change and variation in an urban vernacular. In Trudgill, P. (ed.), *Sociolinguistic patterns in British English*. London: Arnold.

Milroy, J., and L. Milroy. 1993. Mechanisms of change in urban dialects: The role of class, social network, and gender. *International Journal of Applied Linguistics 3.1*: 57–78.

North Carolina Department of Public Instruction. 2005. *Guidelines for testing students identified as limited English proficient*. NC Testing Program, Grades 3–12. Raleigh, NC: State Board of Education Department of Public Instruction: Division of Accountability Services/North Carolina Testing Program. Retrieved from <www.dpi.state.nc.us/docs/accountability/policyoperations/LEPGuidelines_Sept05.pdf> on 9/14/2017.

Ramirez, R. R., and G. Patricia de la Cruz. 2002. *The ispanic population in the United States: March 2002*. Current Population Reports, P20–545. U.S. Census Bureau, Washington, DC.

Rickford, J. 1999. *African American English: Features, evolution, educational implications*. Malden, MA: Blackwell.

Schrank, F. A., K. S. McGrew, M. L. Ruef, C. G. Alvarado, A. F. Muñoz-Sandoval, and R. W. Woodcock. 2005. *Overview and technical supplement: Batería III Woodcock-Muñoz: Assessment Service Bulletin No. 1*. Itasca, IL: Riverside Publishing.

Slomanson, P., and M. Newman. 2004. Peer group identification and variation in New York Latino English laterals. *English World-Wide 25.2*: 199–216.

Sharma, D. 2011. Style repertoire and social change in British Asian English. *Journal of Sociolinguistics 15.4*: 464–492.

Stepler, R., and M. H. Lopez. 2016. U.S. Latino population growth and dispersion has slowed since onset of the great recession. *Pew Research Center*. Retrieved 11/5/2017 from <www.pewhispanic.org/2016/09/08/latino-population-growth-and-dispersion-has-slowed-since-the-onset-of-the-great-recession/> on 8/4/2017.

Weldon, T. 2004. African American English in the middle classes: Exploring the other end of the continuum. Paper presented at NWAV 33, University of Michigan, Ann Arbor, MI.

Wolck, W. 2002. Ethnolects—between bilingualism and urban dialect. In Fishman, J. A. (ed.), *Opportunities and challenges of bilingualism*: 157–170. Berlin: Mouton de Gruyter.

Wolfram, W. 2007. Sociolinguistic folklore in the study of African American English. *Language and Linguistic Compass 1.4*: 292–313.

Wolfram, W., and R. W. Fasold. 1974. *The study of social dialects in the United States*. Englewood Cliffs: Prentice Hall.

Zhang, Q. 2005. A Chinese yuppie in Beijing: Phonological variation and the construction of a new professional identity. *Language in Society 34*: 431–466.

4 A Quantitative Portrait of Ethnolectal Emergence

INT: *So you can be friends with kids from the gangs but not be in a gang yourself?*

Paco: *Mm- yeah. I was in one but I got out.*

INT: *Yeah? What was that like?*

Paco: *Crazy.*

INT: *Were people mad about you getting out? You know, wanting-*

Paco: *Getting out? Yeah.*

INT: *So how did you deal with that?*

Paco: *Huh?*

INT: *How did you deal with that, like-*

Paco: *Nothing. I just said I wanted to get out and that's it.*

INT: *Do you have to- is there . . . like, do you have to tell 'em all, like, "hey, I'm getting out," or do you just stop hanging out with them or-*

Paco: *Just getting out, that's it. They only told me, just, you gotta say that "that's it." They gotta, um, hit you with a bat, and in the face and a lot of stuff . . . and to get in[to] [the gang] too.*

Tobi: *They'll beat you- to get in and to get out.*

INT: *Both ways you get beat.*

Paco: *Yeah.*

4.1 Introduction

This chapter will describe the coding procedures used to analyze unmarked tense in NCHE before going on to present the results of the quantitative analysis in terms of factors described in Chapter 2 (linguistic, social and discourse variables hypothesized to constrain past tense marking). As discussed in Chapter 2, I will use an in-depth analysis of tense unmarking variation to investigate patterns on multiple linguistic levels, including grammar (e.g., verb class), sound (phonological environment), meaning/semantics (lexical aspect) and usage (frequency). This investigation will also outline which social and developmental variables (age, gender, LOR, etc.) correlate with marking patterns for this group of speakers representing a range of proficiency in English and Spanish and differing periods of residency in the US. Finally, I will investigate group accommodation to local patterns in forms of African American English (AAE) via an analysis of CCR for both NCHE and Durham AAE. The processes named in this paragraph—linguistic, developmental and social/local—form the layers of ethnolect emergence in this community, addressing the questions raised in Chapter 1, including: how do NCHE speakers who are emergent bilinguals learn the English(es) of their community? What factors—including the structure of language itself, the time spent in the new community, the stories they tell and the groups they identify with—help predict the kind of English they will end up speaking? And what does this new kind of English tell us about the speech forms emerging in multiethnic, multilingual language learning communities across the US, each of which feature their own heritage languages in contact with English, speakers at varying stages of language development, groups/peers and stories?

4.2 Coding Unmarked Tense

In this section, I will describe the specific coding categories which were used to run the statistical analysis of unmarked tense in Durham NCHE (see note 1 in Chapter 1 for decisions on naming conventions). As mentioned in Chapter 1, tokens of unmarked and marked past tense forms were extracted by listening to audio data that had been digitized and uploaded to the SLAAP database. Once a token was identified, it was transcribed in an Excel sheet and coded for overt tense marking, the dependent variable. The token was then further coded for the following 10 independent variables, the first seven of which are linguistic factors and the last six of which are social factors (Table 4.1):

Table 4.1 Linguistics and social factors coded for unmarked tense in Durham NCHE

FACTOR	CODE
1. Verb Class	a. Suppletive (e.g., *is/was*, *go/went*) b. Doubly marked (e.g.,*leave/left*, *say/said*); c. Internal vowel change, (e.g., *come/came*); d. Change in final segment (e.g., *have/had*, *bend, bent, try, tried*); e. Regular (*-ed*) consonant cluster verbs (e.g., *talk, talked*) f. Weak syllabic (*start/started*) g. Nonverbal/lexical ending in consonant cluster (*best, friend*)

(Continued)

Table 4.1 (Continued)

FACTOR	CODE
2. Phonological Environment	a. _V (*ate and . . .*) b. _C (*ate when. . .*) c. _P(ause) (*ate. Then. . .*)
3. Lexical Aspect	a. Achievement b. Accomplishment c. Activity d. State e. Nonverbal (n/a)
4. Frequency	a. High (top 10% of verbs in corpus) b. Mid (80%–90% percentile) c. Low (all others)
5. Length of Residency (LOR)	Number in years speakers have lived in the US (6-month intervals: 0.5–15.0 years)
6. Interview	Interview name/designation in SLAAP, e.g., dps0271d, dps090d
7. Interviewer(s)	Names/initials of fieldworker(s) conducting the sociolinguistic interview
8. Gender	a. Female b. Male
9. Age	Age in years (year intervals: 9–15 years)
10. School	a. E.K. Powe Elementary b. Chewning Middle c. Rogers-Herr Middle
11. Gang Affiliation (Self- and Teacher Report)	a. Gang-affiliated b. Non-gang-affiliated

Factors 1. and 2., verb class and phonological environment, were discussed in section 2.2 in the context of Wolfram's Vietnamese English studies and Bayley's subsequent Chinese English studies. A few nominal changes were made to the methodologies used in those studies; for example, Wolfram coded speakers into four age groups spanning into adulthood and two LOR groups. In earlier stages of analysis (Callahan 2008), I chose to group speakers into three LOR categories to facilitate GOLDVARB analysis (as this program only admits categorical data), the logistic regression used in this study permitted ages and LORs to be entered as continuous data (i.e., in numeric form).

Tokens that were excluded included negative phrases (*I didn't know/ she didn't talk*), since in English tense is marked on the negative auxiliary and not the main verb. Contracted and zero copula forms (*There's a girl in my class, They 0 so cool*) were excluded as well: though I did observe these forms in past tense environments and in the midst of past tense narratives, it was not possible in these cases to distinguish underlying present tense marking (*is/are*) from underlying past tense marking (*was/were*). One further addition to Wolfram's coding categories was my decision to code for following phonological environment (_C, _V or _P) not only following cluster forms such as *kissed* or *leaned* (which would typically show a phonological effect of reduction preconsonantally), but also for forms that took a replacive final consonant *(agree/agreed, die/died)*.The rationale here was that while Spanish phonotactics do permit postvocalic, word-final alveolar stops (V+*d* as in *verdad* 'truth/true,' *pared* 'wall' and, less often, V+ *t* in non-Spanish (including indigenous) borrowings, e.g., *yogurt, closet, Nayarít* (state in Mexico)), the /-t, -d/ segment itself is reduced or deleted in Spanish in qualitatively different ways. For similar reasons, doubly marked forms (*keep/kept, hear/heard*) were coded for following phonological environment in cases in which the internal vowel change often involved a contrast that does not exist in the Spanish vowel system (i.e., 'keep' and 'kept' exploit the nonnative /i/ vs. /ɛ/ but not 'tell' vs. 'told, in which /ɛ/ might be rendered as [e] but /o/ remains distinct). Finally, in the case of weak syllabic forms (*needed, started*), I also coded for following phonological environment since unstressed syllables in English can be variably reduced or even deleted. When past tense morphology *could* be reduced or deleted in Spanish or English generally, I coded the phonological environment to have a record of possible effects.

4.3 Lexical Aspect

Factor 3. in Table 4.1, lexical aspect, was coded as a property of the verb phrase (VP) as constituted by the main verb and its complements in the sentence, e.g., *get on my nerves* (Jesy, dps0970d), not simply GET. This distinction is necessary since the semantic variable may be coded different depending on the verb's complements: thus, *get on my nerves* was classified as an (atelic/unbounded) activity with no inherent endpoint, whereas *get home* (Fely, dps1271d) was classified as a (telic/bounded) accomplishment. Next, the following tests were applied to classify the sentence into the four relevant categories (Shirai and Andersen 1995: 749):

Step 1: State or nonstate

Does it have a habitual interpretation in simple present tense?

If no —> State (e.g., *I love you*)
If yes —> Nonstate (e.g., *I eat bread*) —> Go to Step 2

Step 2: Activity or nonactivity

Does 'X is Ving' entail 'X has Ved' without an iterative/habitual meaning? In other words, if you stop in the middle of Ving, have you done the act of V?

If yes —> Activity (e.g., *run*)
If no —> Nonactivity (e.g., *run a mile*) —> Go to Step 3

Step 3: Accomplishment or achievement

[If test (a) does not work, apply test (b), and possibly (c).]

a. If 'X Ved in Y time (e.g., 10 minutes),' then 'X was Ving during that time.'

If yes —> Accomplishment (e.g., *He painted a picture.*)
If no —> Achievement (e.g., *He noticed a picture*)

b. Is there ambiguity with almost?

If yes —> Accomplishment (e.g., *He almost painted a picture* has two readings: he almost started to paint a picture/he almost finished painting a picture.)
If no —> Achievement (e.g., *He almost noticed a picture* has only one reading.)

c. 'X will VP in Y time' (e.g., 10 minutes) = 'X will VP after Y time.' If no —> Accomplishment
d. If yes —> Achievement

Finally, to assess the effect of telicity overall (i.e., whether or not the VP has an inherent, natural endpoint), states and activities were further coded as one category (telic predicates) and accomplishment and achievements were similarly coded into one category (atelic predicates).

4.4   Discourse Structure

In terms of discourse (narrative) structure, it was necessary to consider the potential effects of conversational functions speakers may use to tell the story itself—to bring it to life for their audience. As noted in Chapter 1, some studies, beginning with Kumpf (1984), approached tense marking patterns in second-language narratives by comparing unmarked forms with the use of the so-called historical or conversational present in order to account for this pragmatic/storytelling function. Here, the use of the conversational present (CP) occurs when the story's verb form refers to events that are semantically past;

however, the speaker describes them in the present tense as a pragmatic device to lend a sense of 'immediacy' to his narrative. The following excerpt gives an example of a narrative from high-proficiency speaker Julio (dps0402d, 254s):

Julio: In "America's Funniest Video," have y'all seen that show?
INT 1:   Uh-huh.
Julio: There was this man, he was tryin to- tryin to sell this cat. And he was, he was sayin like um, on camera, he was sayin that there wa- thi- that would be the nic- that was the nicest cat he's ever known. *And then, when he **takes** him out of the bag, or the box, the box I mean, he **bites** him on the leg.*
INT 1:   <gasp>
INT 2:   <laughs>
Julio: . . . and then he say he'd be the nicest cat in the world.

The two phrases in which Julio uses the CP (in *takes* and *bites*) are in bold in this dialogue ('*when he **takes** him out of the. . . box. . . he **bites** him on the leg*"). Julio's use of the CP is typical in that he uses it to deliver the 'punchline' of his anecdote, which is simultaneously the climax of his oral narrative as a complicating action. The joke is funny since it is ironic that the "nicest cat [the man] has ever known" would bite its owner in the cat's video debut; here, the CP highlights the chunk of narrative Julio's speakers must attend to in order to 'get' the joke. Though his story is initially framed as occurring in the past in an opening clause that has tense marked on its narrative 'head' ("There **was** this man. . . "), Julio exploits explicit present tense morphology (3rd sg. -s) to move the most important part of his story forward. After it is clear that his joke has succeeded with the audience ("INT 1: <gasp>/INT 2: <laughs>"), Julio shifts back into using unmarked past tense ". . . and then he say he'd be the nicest cat in the world").

As in some previous analyses of unmarked tense variation, Julio's principled, native speaker-like use of CP (with or without 'tell-tale' 3rd sg. marking) was not immediately observed for the beginning language learners in this study. At first glance, these speakers seem not to have (yet) acquired this particular discourse function. The lowest proficiency speakers did use alternate paralinguistic and linguistic cues like increased volume, intonation contours and eye contact to mark narrative functions; however, they did not seem to use CP, at least in the paradigmatic sense. The following excerpt features Enrique, a speaker who has lived in the US less than one year, one of the lowest LORs in this study. This excerpt gives a sense of the character of tense alternations that occur at the very beginning language learner narratives in the study. Enrique (dps049d/1580s) describes to the interviewer what happened on a recent field trip to Washington, DC:

Enrique: I **look** the airplane and. . . .
INT: At the museum?
Enrique: Uh-huh, and . . . I **look** the animals . . . I **look** the animals . . . I
              go to . . . *fui a comprar cosas* in *una tienda* ('I went to buy some
              things in a store').

The interviewees in this study, especially the lower proficiency speakers, were made aware (in most English interviews) that if they didn't know a word in English, they could say it in Spanish. Here, Enrique uses a code switch (*fui a comprar cosas* in *una tienda* 'I went to buy some things in a store') as a strategy to move the events of his narrative forward and keep the attention of his audience (a bilingual fieldworker).

   Initially, these paralinguistic cues seemed to correlate more closely with the function served by CP in native (MAE) speech. However, to test formally for the patterning of conversational present, narratives from 15 of the low- to mid-proficiency speakers were transcribed and coded for the foregrounding vs. backgrounding function vs. tense unmarking. The first completed narrative to appear after the first five minutes of the interview was transcribed and coded. Here, for example, Alejo (dps049/345s), a mid-proficiency speaker, recounts what happened in a movie he recently saw:

	F	B
INT: What happened?		
Alejo: *There's a rat that—it's in—I don't remember—he's in another state.*		
*And then he—another rat **come** for the—*	X	
can I say it in Spanish, that word? From the *taza*. . . from the thing that—		
INT: The spoon? The cup, I mean, the cup? Alejo: no, where you pee.		
INT: Oh, the toilet? Alejo: Yes.		
INT: Uh-huh.		
Alejo: *A rat **come** from over there.* INT: Uh-huh.	X	
Alejo: *and the rat that **was** in the other state—*		X
*he **say** "you need to get out of here."*	X	
*And he **say** "No."*	X	
*"Do you have TV?" And he **say** "yes."*		
*And then the rat that **come** from the toil et **say** , "Oh my God, look at this monster!"*	X	
*That **was** a big TV.*		X
*And then, he **say** "Do you wanna. . . bañarte en el jacuzzi?"*	X	
INT: <laughs> Uh-huh.		
Alejo:*. . . and that **was** the toilet.*		X
*And he **say** "Sure."*	X	

	F	B
*And then he **say** "OK, go down. Go down."*	X	
*And he **say** "OK, here I'm going. . . One, two—wait!"*	X	
*And then he **drove** the other rat to the water*	X	
*and he **go** down, down*	X	
and there was a big city, like big city. INT: Under the water?		X
Alejo: *Yes. The rats **made** a city.*		X
And there was a—		
*The rat **was** a girl.*		X
*And another rats **want** to kill her. Another rats.*		X
*And he **have** a diamond.*		X
*That's why they **want** to kill her.*		X
*But she **want** to escape.*		X
*And the guy that **come** down*		X
*he **say***	X	
*he **want** to get to hisselfs [sic] again*		X
And the rat say—		
*the girl **say** , "I'm sorry. I have m—problems."*	X	
*And the rat **say** "Please, please. I have a lot of diamonds up there."*	X	
And. . . I don't remember.		

The clauses that form Alejo's narrative are italicized. The verbs in bold were considered candidates for the unmarking analysis. When it could not be determined if the tense was present or past tense (*There's*, *It's*) or if the clause/verb form did not form part of the narrative (e.g., *where you pee*, as an 'aside' when Alejo asks for clarification), the token was excluded from the analysis. In addition, if a clause was a false start (*And there was a—*, *he say—*) it was excluded. A clause that "pushed the event line forward" (Kumpf 1984: 141) was coded as a foreground clause; correspondingly; background clauses were defined as those that "set the scene, make digressions, change the normal sequence of events, or give evaluative remarks" (1984: 141). These procedures for coding foreground vs. background clauses are identical to the methods used in the 1980s Vietnamese English tense unmarking studies that examined the use of CP (Wolfram and Hatfield 1984; Wolfram and Hatfield 1984).

4.5 Other Exclusions

I excluded tokens from the analysis if they seemed to be lexicalized, including tokens 'and' and 'just.' I initially noticed very few full clusters at the ends of these words; therefore, during coding of the first 31 speakers, I coded the first five instances of each token and spot-checked the remainder of each interview. I did not transcribe a single unreduced form in this subsample of 155 cases; therefore I hypothesized that these entries may not be variable for many speakers (i.e., they are acquired without the final segment).

4.6   Statistical Methods

Initially, basic graphs (e.g., scatterplots; raw incidence of verb marking by speaker, interview or age) and descriptive statistics (e.g., cross tabulation of phonological environment vs. marking; verb frequency histograms) were used to visualize data and check for obvious interactions among factors. This initial, exploratory phase of analysis was carried out using the same program in which the data were tabulated and coded, Microsoft® Excel® version 2010 (version 14.0 for Windows).

Second, a logistic regression using the software program SPSS Statistics (SPSS 21 for Windows) was used to investigate the constraints on tense marking patterns in terms of the independent factors 1–12, listed in Table 4.1; for example, as measured by standard correlation statistics (e.g., Pearson's *r and corresponding significance level p*). The initial regression coded linguistic factors 1.–6. (verb class, phonological environment, lexical aspect, embedded or auxiliary status of verb, frequency class) and social factors 8., 9., 10., and 12. (interview, interviewer(s), gender, and school) as nominal/categorical variables. Only two factors, 7. (length of residency) and 11. (school) were entered as continuous variables.

Subsequent analyses were planned, as needed, with re-codings of the independent factors as entered. For example, in subsequent runs, frequency was reconsidered a continuous measure vs. a categorical one (incidence proportion vs. categories high/medium/low)[1] to identify the best-fitting model. These decisions and their rationale are discussed in detail in section 5.3.5. Finally, in some cases where the graphing functionality or SPSS was limited, the analyses were run in the statistical environment R (version 2.15.1 for Windows) using package 'nlme,' designed for fitting linear mixed-effects models.

Given this overview of the Durham site, speech community and speakers (sections 3.0–3.3) as well as documentation of coding procedures for both the linguistic and social categories (4.1–4.5) and description of statistical methods (4.6), we will move on to section 4.7, which presents the results of the study.

4.7   Results

In this section, I will present the results of the statistical analyses described in section 4.3 in both descriptive terms (by laying out the patterns present in the data) as well as in predictive terms (by accounting for correlations in the dependent variable and sociolinguistic factors, including co-functioning of constraints at multiple linguistic levels). To begin the section, I will comment on overall distribution of marked tokens for tense in the data, then present the overall results of logistic regressions analyses run on each of four linguistic or internal factors in the model (phonological environment, verb class, lexical aspect and frequency), and provide guidelines for interpreting these statistics. After this overall preview of the results of the internal factors, I will examine in detail each linguistic factor individually. Next, I will discuss the influence of discourse/narrative context on unmarking patterns by presenting the results of a subsample of the data that was coded for foregrounding vs. backgrounding function. Finally, I will present the results for each of the social factors hypothesized to correlate with unmarking (LOR,[2] age, school, gender, country of origin, literacy in English/Spanish and gang affiliation) and discuss in detail the effect of LOR in relation to tense unmarking.

4.7.1 Overall Distribution of Tokens

Of the 2012 total nominal and verbal tokens (i.e., marked and unmarked) produced by all speakers in the study, the mean number of tokens produced per speaker was 46 (median = 36), with the speakers producing the fewest tokens (Anabel and George, each with a LOR = <1 year) producing only one token each and the speaker producing the most tokens (Marisa) producing a maximum of 164 tokens. The spread for quantity of tokens produced was fairly high (standard deviation = 40.5), though, interestingly, there was a low correlation (r = .23) between length of residency and number of tokens produced: in other words, low LOR didn't necessarily keep speakers from talking. In fact, of the four speakers who produced over 100 tokens each, one had been in the US only two years (Marisa; n =164) and the other for four years (Fely; n =106). Figure 4.1

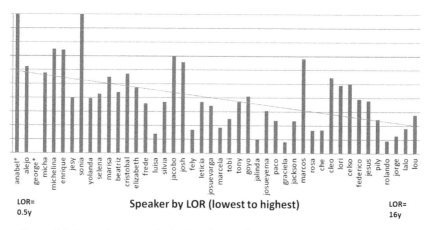

LOR=
0.5y

Speaker by LOR (lowest to highest)

LOR=
16y

Figure 4.1 Percentage unmarked tokens by speaker

lists percentage of unmarked tense for all 44 speakers in the study, with names of speakers provided for reference. As we might expect, there is a wide spread, with some speakers (e.g., Cleo, LOR = 10; Selena; LOR = 2) marking a relatively low number of tokens and other speakers (Tony, LOR = 16) marking almost all his tokens.

4.7.2 Results by Linguistic Factor Group

Table 4.2 shows the results of logistic regressions run on each of the main linguistic factors in the model, demonstrating that all four (phonological environment, verb class, lexical aspect and frequency) correlate significantly with rates of past tense marking.

4.7.3 Interpretation of Logistic Regression Statistics

Before investigating these initial results further, it may be useful to provide a brief explanation of the meaning of each statistic given in Table 4.2 since researchers across fields (SLA, sociolinguistics, etc.) may have varying degrees of familiarity with statistical analysis of linguistic data. In broad terms, the individual figures shown in Table 4.2 demonstrate, in general,

Table 4.2 Logistic regression results for linguistic (internal) factors

	β	χ^2 (Model)	−2 Log Likelihood	Sig.	Pseudo (Nagelkerke) R^2
1. Phonological Environment		28.6	1272.951	p < .000	.04
a. Consonant	−0.515				
b. Pause	−1.011				
c. Vowel [ref]					
2. Verb Class		441.6	2097.623	p < .000	.28
a. Cluster verb (picked)	−0.520				
b. Final replacive C (had)	0.676				
c. Doubly marked (told)	0.924				
d. Vowel change (came)	1.102				
e. Suppletive (went)	2.179				
Weak syllabic (wanted) [ref]					
3. Lexical Aspect		336.5	2298.175	p < .000	.21
a. Accomplishment	0.925				
b. Achievement	1.188				
c. State	1.706				
Activity [ref]					
4. Frequency	.010	355.7	2268.100	p < .000	.22
5. LOR	.093	187.5	2566.011	p < .000	.05

whether the relationships observed between each factor and the incidence of unmarked tense are due to chance or not. First, the chi-square statistic (χ^2), used frequently in studies of categorical/structural variation, provides a measure of the likelihood that each factor (phonological environment, verb class, etc.) functions independently from the occurrence of unmarked tense in this data set: it describes 'goodness of fit' in terms of a comparison between the distribution we would expect if the variables were entirely independent from the phenomenon under investigation and the actual data distribution we observe (in terms of the number of unmarked vs. marked forms with respect to each factor previously mentioned, 1.–4.). Here, the greater the chi-square statistic, the greater the likelihood that the variables (e.g., phonological environment vs. marking patterns) are actually dependent in their functioning—and the *less* likely that the null hypothesis, the assumption of no effect, or random variation is correct.

Ultimately, we can use the chi-square statistic, in conjunction with the number of degrees of freedom (a measure of independence of the various factors: from a data table, we would calculate (R - 1) * (C - 1) where R = number of rows and C = number of columns) to consult a standard normal distribution table in order to look up an approximate probability, or p-value. Here, a value of .052 would mean, more or less, that *if* the data distribution is in fact simply due to chance, one would have (roughly) a 5.2% chance of finding a result as extreme as the one in a given data set. In other words, the null hypothesis (the functioning of random chance) is about 5.2% likely to be correct. It follows that a lower p-value can point to the likelihood of a stronger relationship among the factors.

The -2 log likelihood figure also compares the fit of two models, one of which assumes the null hypothesis is correct and the other which follows the study hypothesis (e.g., 'phonological environment correlates in a statistically significant way with unmarked tense').[3] Similar to a chi-square statistic, the -2 log likelihood is an index of how unlikely it is that a particular arrangement of data might be produced simply due to chance (i.e., in a universe where none of the hypothesized constraints actually predicted the variation under investigation).

The final statistic, a pseudo-R-squared (R^2), is not widely used in studies of (categorical) variation but is useful here since the traditional R-squared itself is widely used and recognized. Also known as the 'coefficient of determination,' a traditional R-squared value measures, in general, the proportion of variance accounted for by a researcher's model. Typically, R-squared ranges from 0 to 1.0, with values closer to 1 indicating a better fit of the model to the variation in the data (we could say, in turn, that an R-squared value of .12 accounts, roughly, for about 12% of the variation present in the data). It is important to note here that this traditional R-squared measure is used only with *continuous* variation (e.g., fundamental frequency, which might range in a given sociolinguistic study, from 100Hz to 200Hz), not *categorical* variation where, for example, only two discrete values are possible (0 = unmarked/1 = marked with nothing in between). However, in order to test goodness of fit in a general way for models that attempt to predict categorical variation, statisticians have developed pseudo-R-squared measures, which use a similar scale, from 0 to 1, with higher values indicating better model fit; this measure is especially useful in comparing effects within one model (i.e., pseudo-R-squared values can be meaningfully compared with each other within one analysis, but not as readily across alternate models with different sets of factors.

4.7.4   *Phonological Environment*

Figure 4.2 shows raw counts of the phonological variable of consonant cluster reduction (CCR), or *-t/d* absence, on verbal tokens that are candidates for the unmarking process (that is, as discussed in sections 2.8.2 and 4.2, all cases of past tense that were potentially formed through the addition of /t/ or /d/ that might result in a consonant cluster (e.g., *missed*) as well as monomorphemes whose final syllable ended in a cluster (*mist*)).

Setting the Y axis equal to count vs. percentage allows us to see the raw totals of kinds of verbs, marked and unmarked in the data, relative to each other. The pattern observed here reflects the trend that has been widely demonstrated in studies of CCR in both native and learner English speech communities: preconsonantal tokens favor the process of reduction (a token

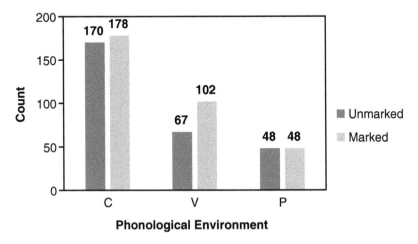

Figure 4.2 Raw counts of—t/-d absence by phonological environment

like 'picked through' is reduced most often) and prevocalic tokens disfavor it ('picked up' is reduced least often). Rates for prepausal tokens ('the one I picked'), however, which usually fall between the two levels, are lower than either preconsonantal or prevocalic tokens. For now, we will lay aside this effect and return to the discussion later vis-à-vis similar effects in local varieties of African American English later, in this chapter.

4.7.5 Lexical Aspect

Figure 4.3 shows the results for past tense marking and lexical aspect based on the definitions of these different categories proposed in section 2.6.1.

First, we can see that there are more marked tokens overall than unmarked: most verbs in the data set are marked with Standard English type past tense marking. Second, the aspect variable is marked at the relative rates we would expect, with telic predicates marked overall relatively more often than atelic predicates—with the exception of states, which are apparently marked at rates twice as high as the trailing category, accomplishments. This is a surprising result since we would expect that statives would be highly unmarked if lexical aspect does in fact influence marking patterns. However, there is evidence that this effect appears to be at least partially lexically based: one token type, the copula, accounts for almost 17% of the total Ns in the data: copula is the most frequent token type overall. Furthermore, of the 675 tokens that describe a state (in addition to copula, verbs like 'have,' 'want,' and 'believe'), a full 359, or 53%, are copula tokens. Of these copula

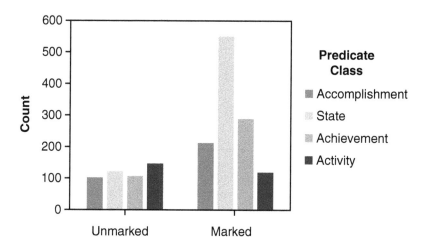

Figure 4.3 Raw counts of surface past tense marking by lexical aspect

tokens, an overwhelming majority, or 97%, are marked—thus, copula is almost categorically marked and makes up over half of the stative tokens.

These high rates of copula marking (along with high incidence of copula itself) have also been found in previous studies of English interlanguage variation: Kumpf (1984), in the study described in section 2.5.1, found that over half her stative tokens are copula and that, furthermore, copula is tensed 100% of the time. Ellis (1987), in an analysis of style-shifting among 17 EFL university students, found that copula marking showed intermediate effects between that of regular verbs and irregulars.

When Ellis's subjects (low-intermediate learners from mixed language backgrounds) were given extra planning time to orally narrate the events they saw in a sequence of pictures, the planned (spoken) narratives showed a higher incidence of copula marking, from 60% to 75% ($\chi^2 = 4.36$; $p < .05$).[4] Bayley (1991) does not report especially high levels of copula marking in his Chinese English studies, but does justify bifurcating copula into two different factor groups in his VARBRUL analysis, since all forms of copula except for 1st singular pattern with internal vowel change forms over suppletives (i.e., *is—> was* is more similar to *come—> came* than, say, *go—> went*).[5] In any case, there is sufficient evidence to consider copula as a class (or classes) unto itself in studies of English interlanguage variation. Indeed, as shown in Figure 4.4, when state/copula tokens are excluded, marking patterns at all levels of proficiency follow the prediction for marking by lexical aspect, where activities are marked less often than achievements, though the lowest LOR speakers mark significantly fewer verbal tokens overall.

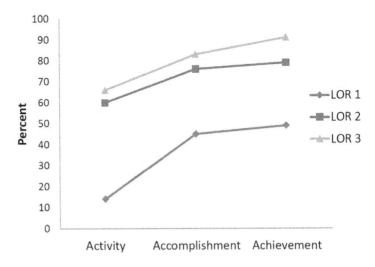

Figure 4.4 Percentage of past tense marking by lexical aspect (copula excluded)

4.7.6   Verb Class

The saliency hierarchy, represented by verb class, by contrast, does follow the expected rank order observed in previous studies, with a reverse in doubly marked and internal vowel change type verbs (Figure 4.5).

Here, the regular verbs—weak syllabic 'wanted' and regular cluster 'picked' and 'leaned'—share relatively more segments with their stem, making them less phonetically salient to learners.[6] By contrast, doubly marked forms like *tell—> told* and suppletive forms like *go—> went* show markedly higher rates of marking, though they also represent the majority of tokens overall.

Furthermore, overall rates of marking by verb class show sensitivity to phonetic salience at all proficiency levels, from speakers who have lived in the US for one to three years (LOR 1) to speakers who have lived in the US for six or more (LOR 3) (Figure 4.6).

When the results are articulated by proficiency, it becomes evident that the very beginning language learners (LOR 1: 1–3 years) do narrowly follow the saliency hierarchy as-is, and the reversal in doubly marked and internal vowel change verbs happens (though not at dramatic levels) in the latter two LOR periods. However, overall, we can identify two main trends: 1) marking remains lower overall at the lower proficiency levels and higher overall at the higher proficiency levels, regardless of verb class; and 2) rates of marking by verb class tend to stabilize at the higher proficiency levels, though sensitivity to the saliency hierarchy remains.

To round out a discussion of verb class, we will consider a comparison of three previous studies of variation in past tense marking in learner English with the results from this study. Here, Figure 4.7 shows the results of the present study (Durham Hispanic English) alongside Wolfram's and

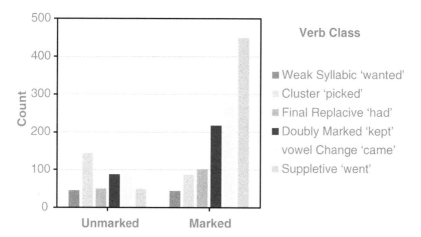

Figure 4.5 Raw counts of past tense marking by verb class

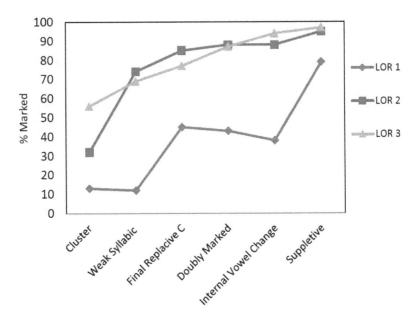

Figure 4.6 Percentage of past tense marking by verb class

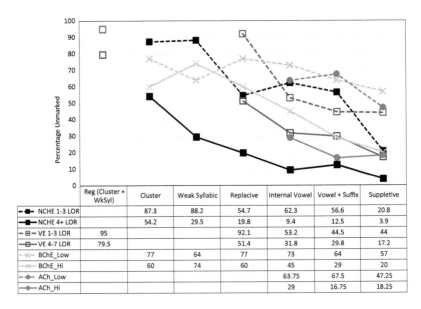

	Reg (Cluster + WkSyl)	Cluster	Weak Syllabic	Replacive	Internal Vowel	Vowel + Suffix	Suppletive
NCHE 1-3 LOR		87.3	88.2	54.7	62.3	56.6	20.8
NCHE 4+ LOR		54.2	29.5	19.8	9.4	12.5	3.9
VE 1-3 LOR	95			92.1	53.2	44.5	44
VE 4-7 LOR	79.5			51.4	31.8	29.8	17.2
BChE_Low		77	64	77	73	64	57
BChE_Hi		60	74	60	45	29	20
ACh_Low					63.75	67.5	47.25
ACh_Hi					29	16.75	18.25

Figure 4.7 Percentage of unmarking by verb class and proficiency for three studies of English interlanguage

Hatfield's (1984) adult Vietnamese English speakers, Bayley's (1991) young adult Chinese English speakers and Adamson's (2009) elementary-aged Chinese English speakers.

As mentioned in section 4.7.2, Bayley ultimately combines into classes his 1a. strong verbs (vowel change: *come—> came*) and 1b. copula other than 1st singular (*is—> was*) as well as 2a. replacives (send—> *sent*) and 2b. weak nonsyllabics (*walk—> walked*), accounting for the blank cells in the table below the results. Wolfram and Hatfield, similarly, combine regular verbs into one class (cluster verbs and weak syllabics), and Adamson only considers three categories in his study (vowel change, replacives and suppletives).

Despite the differing methodological conventions, however, the graph illustrates the striking effect of phonetic saliency across language learning communities and proficiency levels. The main difference that can be observed for Durham HE is the low overall rates of unmarking by the high-proficiency speakers; as a group, these speakers mark many more verbal tokens than their language learning cohorts in the other three studies (staying below 50% unmarking for all verb classes except for cluster verbs). One fundamental difference in the overall profile of each community in the comparison is that the Durham speech community includes both recent immigrants as well as native speakers whereas Wolfram's and Hatfield's high-proficiency category topped out at seven years, Bayley's highest proficiency speaker (Guo Chang) had been in the US only 54 months, and Adamson's longitudinal study included children in their first three years of residence in the US.

It is worth noting, however, that the native/nonnative distinction in Durham, which may in general seem very primary, does not play out in clear-cut terms. Linguistically speaking, of the 11 US-born speakers in the study (Lou, Lalo, Pily, Jesús, Federico, Jorge, Rolando, Lori, Micha, Michelina, Alejo), all used the unmarking process in at least one noncluster verb (i.e., outside of environments where the process could simply be attributed to phonological reduction). Lori, who is 12-years old, was born in North Carolina, left at age 5 to live in the Mexico City and returned to the US at age 7 (when, she says, she "forgot all her English"). Alejo, 9, was born in Pennsylvania where his mother had family, attended 1st through 4th grade in Michoacán (Mexico) and had only recently returned to the US at the time of the study. Lou, one of the oldest speakers in the study at 16, was born in Waco, TX, lived across the border in Mexico until he was 1-years old, then moved with his family to Rougemont, NC.

The native/nonnative distinction also does not play out as one might think in social space (in terms of ties to home and vacations abroad). In my experience as a teacher, it was often harder for the foreign-born, undocumented students to travel with their families outside the US since they would have to risk another perilous 'crossing' to re-enter. Thus, some students who were born in the US actually maintained closer ties with Spanish-speaking family outside the US and were able to visit them more frequently and freely. Moreover, in the everyday, the US-born and non-US-born students spent much of their daily schedule together: all 11 speakers attended regular ESL classes with their lower proficiency peers, whether in a stand-alone class (a period during the middle school day) or during a 'pull out' session with their elementary school ESL teacher. Thus, the lines between 'native' and 'nonnative' speaker of English were often blurred in both linguistic terms (successive rates of unmarking) as well as in social (institutional, political) terms. The implication of this finding for policy and pedagogy applications will be discussed in Chapter 5.

4.8   Frequency

Much of the recent 'usage-' or 'exemplar-based' (Bybee 2001) work on the role of frequency in linguistic variation has been done on phonological structures like variable /s/-reduction in Spanish (Brown and Cacoullos 2002), variable coronal stop deletion in English or *t-to-r* in English (Clark and Watson 2011). Erker and Guy (2012), in a frequency-based study of variable subject personal pronoun expression in Spanish, present a number of distinct issues at stake in quantifying usage-based effects in studies of syntactic variation. The data in this study follow the first (typical) trend they describe: there are many highly frequent tokens (*be, friend*) and, conversely, few very rare tokens (*betray, scientist*), presenting issues for a statistical analysis that is very sensitive to sample size. Other issues include whether to consider verbs as abstract units or parts of collocations with their objects (*get X* vs. collocations like *get-mad* vs. *get-through*, etc.), whether to use local or global corpora, whether to consider frequency as a continuous vs. categorical constraint, and whether to consider frequency as a traditional 'factor group' at all, or one that may intersect in meaningful ways with independently functioning sociolinguistic constraints. Finally, there is the question of whether frequency resists or accelerates change, as with morphological generalization. Poplack (2001), for example, showed that for variation in the subjunctive in Canadian French, very high-frequency verbs like *falloir* preserved older forms. Similarly, the well-known pattern in the history of English preterit is a trend from strong forms ('dreamt,' 'dove') to weak forms ('dreamed,' 'dived') based on high token frequency and low token type.

In this study, I followed Erker and Guy (2012) in coding all data by raw frequency count (a token that occurred 15 times received a frequency rating of 15) and designating high-frequency tokens as ones that occurred in the top 1% of all verbal tokens. In our data set of 2012 tokens, this 1% threshold occurred at n = 20 (that is, if a token occurred 20 times or more, it was categorized as a high-frequency token). For phrasal verbs ('get ahead' vs. 'get through') I coded the verb and its complement. Figure 4.8 illustrates

Figure 4.8 Token by raw frequency with reference line for high vs. low

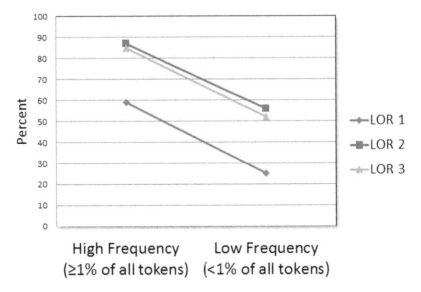

Figure 4.9 Percentage of marking by frequency and LOR

the distribution of all verbs in the data with a reference line at n = 20, the cut-off point designated for high vs. low frequency.

As expected, learners mark high-frequency tokens (like *die, win* and *look*) at higher rates at all proficiency levels as compared to low-frequency items (like *blame, switch* or *cuss*) (Figure 4.9).

However, this effect is not so straightforward. Figure 4.10 demonstrates how frequency itself is articulated by verb class.

The top half of Figure 4.9 illustrates that at all levels of proficiency, suppletives (the most commonly verbs used overall) are employed consistently by speakers at all LOR points at rates over three times that of the other verb classes. As the most phonetically distinct type of verb, indeed, they must be frequent to resist the forces of leveling or generalization over time: in Bybee's (2001) terms, they have increased lexical strength. Bybee also notes that highly frequent or entrenched words and phrases tend to be cognitively stored unanalyzed—which, I would argue, correspondingly makes them easy to learn and access for language learners.

4.9   Results by Discourse Factor Group

A subsample of 12 speakers was chosen for the analysis of unmarked tense by discourse/narrative structure factor to test the hypothesis described in sections 2.3 and 4.7.4 that past marking is sensitive to foregrounding vs.

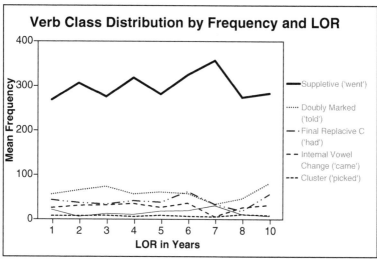

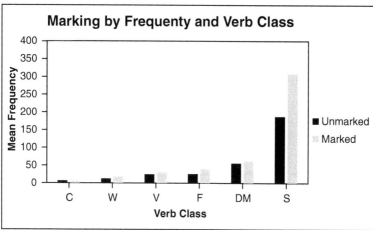

Figure 4.10 Verb class by frequency and LOR

backgrounding function. The first narrative of each of the speakers' interview that contained five or more verbal tokens in obligatory past tense contexts (n = 191) was transcribed and coded according to the procedures outlined in 4.7.4. The results are shown in Figure 4.11.

Though this sample is limited, the overall trend is towards more marking in background clauses ($\chi^2 = 12.28$; $p < .05$): all but two speakers, Jorge and Alejo, categorically marked background clauses. However, the frequency

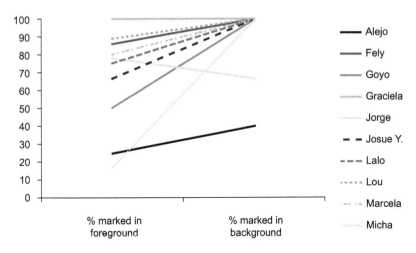

Figure 4.11 Percentage of past tense marking by speaker and narrative function (foreground vs. background)

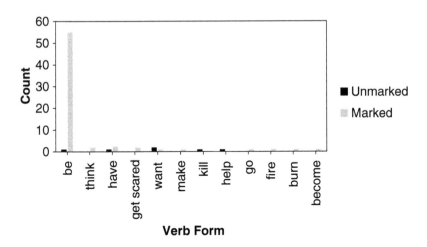

Figure 4.12 Background forms and marking

effect described in section 4.8 was identified for this variable as well: of the background clauses, over 80% (58/72) were copula tokens (Figure 4.12); only 6/116 foreground tokens were copula tokens and all were marked (Figure 4.13).

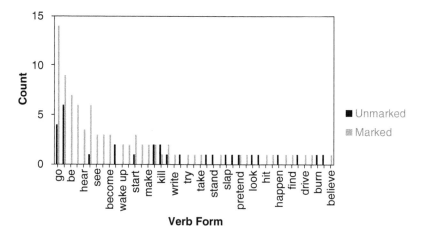

Figure 4.13 Foreground forms and marking

A few examples of the pattern, where copula tokens are used in backgrounds and are marked at high levels, are given below:[7]

1. Pily/091d: *One time I got really scared (.) it was in El Salvador (.) I was at the park . . .*
2. Jorge/dps041d: *Last time I visit (.) was when I was five (.) I want to go visit—a doctor. . . .*
3. Jorge Y./dps0550d: *[Describing a video game he played with a friend] the mission was to—I don't remember but it was something to do with hippies. . . .*
4. Marcela/dps058: *We went like to a yard sale (.) there was—like toys (.) and we buyed it for him [her dog] . . .*

Copula is used the majority of the time for background functions like 'setting the stage' for the events in a storyline, as in 1.–4. Adamson (2009) observed a similar effect in his Chinese English data, where by far the most common background verb was the copula. He notes that since background clauses are not absolutely required in narrative discourse for young speakers (Aksu-Koc and von Stuttenheim 1994 cited in Adamson 2009), the speaker has the freedom to use familiar verbs, whereas in the foreground they are constrained to use particular verbs that describe the events in a particular storyline. In our subsample, there may be some limited evidence to support this account, since Micha and Alejo, both beginning language learners (LOR = 1), also had the lowest rates of foreground marking, however the sample is too limited to draw any definitive conclusions. If anything, there is evidence for copula-heavy backgrounding and marking-heavy copulas in the context of more marking overall in the background for all verbs.

4.10 Results by Social Factor Group

Not unexpectedly, there were highly significant correlations between many of the social factors selected as independent variables, most prominently with LOR. Specifically, collinearity occurred with LOR and the following factors:[8] age ($r = .50$; $p < .000$), gender ($\chi^2 = 1034.2$; $p < .000$), country of birth ($\chi^2 = 2326.3$; $p < .000$), language in which learned to read ($\chi^2 = 3433.2$; $p < .000$), gang affiliation ($\chi^2 = 810.6$; $p < .000$) and school ($\chi^2 = 1641.3$; $p < .000$). Highly significant correlations also occurred with the category gender itself, including age ($\chi^2 = 713.921$; $p < .000$), language in which learned to read ($\chi^2 = 2198.1$; $p < .000$), country of birth ($\chi^2 = 2040$; $p < .000$) and gang affiliation ($\chi^2 = 2326.16$; $p < .000$).

Ultimately, however, there was no need to investigate further the relationships between social factors themselves, since a logistic regression with all social factors included (5–10 in Table 4.4) demonstrated that only one showed a significant relationship with the occurrence of unmarked tense, LOR ($p < .001$).[9] Figure 4.14 shows the general downward trend of the unmarking effect with respect to LOR.

Figure 4.14 demonstrates that speakers are most likely to unmark their verbs during their first 2 years living in the US; during this period, speakers will produce a zero-marked past tense verb nearly 6 times out of every 10. After this initial two-year period, rates of unmarking plummet to a low of 22% by LOR 4. The sharp falls at LOR 7 and 12 may not be representative of the overall trend since those time points represent limited numbers of speakers: only 2 speakers, Marcela and Rosa, represent LOR 7 and, together, only produce 12 tokens, the lowest quantity of any LOR time point. Similarly, LOR 12 is represented by one speaker, Rolando, who produces 22 tokens, and LOR 8 is represented by only four speakers (Marcos, Goyo, Rosa and Jackson), who produce only 82 tokens. Thus, the LOR cells (LOR 7, 12 and 8) that exhibit sharp up or down trends are in fact the least representative of all the time points in the data.

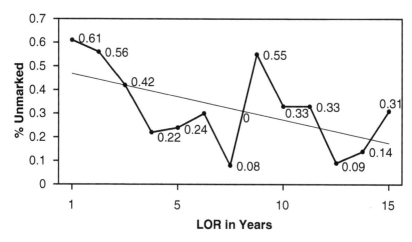

Figure 4.14 Percentage of past tense marking by speaker LOR

4.11 NCHE in the Community Context: Contact with AAE

At this point, it is worth taking note that of the eight independent social factors coded in this analysis, only one developmentally linked factor, LOR, shows significant effects for the unmarking variable. This question—why no social factors, apart from LOR, seem to drive this process—deserves serious examination.

In section 3.1, I discussed how the phonological process of CCR correlates with particular patterns of social category membership in specific communities—for example, the variable shows uniform constraints (e.g., morphemic status vs. phonological environment) that occur in different rank orders, a pattern that has been reliably replicated in many studies over the past four decades. In this section I will return to a discussion of CCR both in Durham HE and AAE in order to explore patterns of social accommodation vs. differentiation in this emerging dialect. Beyond its scholarly value as firsthand evidence of dialect emergence, a clear understanding of the operation of phonological and grammatical variables (CCR in conjunction with past tense unmarking) has real-world implications. These linguistic and social processes have direct effects on the school experience of developing HE speakers, such as in the context of standardized testing designed with Standard English norms. Thus, this section will provide a description of the convergence and divergence of HE in terms of linguistic constraints that have been typically studied for native varieties of English. Chapter 5 will discuss relevant pedagogical applications of the general findings for both CCR and unmarked tense. Finally, Chapter 7 will provide directions for future research and general conclusions for the study as a whole.

4.11.1   AAE Contact Features

Before discussing the quantitative results for CCR, I will provide a sample of some of the AAE features that were observed in the speech of HE speakers in the study (Table 4.3).[10] These examples occurred during the

Table 4.3 AAE features in Durham HE

Feature	Speaker/ Interview	Example
1. Possessive Pronoun Double Marking	Luisa/ dps0280d:	Luisa: We made this friendship bracelet, but I forgot **mines.**
2. Habitual 'be' (Plus Lexical 'playin')	Lalo/ dps0730d	Lalo: **[She be doin a]** lot of things to me. A lot of—private things too.
	Goyo/ dps0080d	Goyo: My brother, he drives. He be—he dr— he be—**we be drivin** over here.
3. Demonstrative Them + Plural Noun	Goyo/ dps0080d	Goyo: And you know, they have **them bumps** in Mexico—like in some streets?
	Che/ dps1080d	Che: [talking about his uncle getting a prize at the Fair] He had one of them—**them— whatchamacallit things.**
4. a' + V-initial noun	Fely/dps1271	Fely:. . . because, um, **a evil man**, I don't remember his name, he was trying to become king.
5. Copula Absence	Marcos/ dps0110d	Marcos:. . . cause they 0 racist.
	Che/ dps1080d	Che: Um, my little sister. . . she 0 about to be nine- no, ten.
6. Preterit 'had'	Che/ dps1080d	INT: [Ghost stories, that's what we were talking] [[about.]] Che: [[Mm?]] INT: So you don't know anybody who's ever seen- seen a ghost? No? Che: <sniff> <creak> Wait, my uncle. FW: Your uncle, that's who it was. Will you [tell that] story again? Che: That's different. <cough> <inhale> He **had** said that he- he saw a ghost. And then <creak> He said- he said something about um—<inhale> that the ghost said <creak> said "Make a wish" [story continues]

Feature	Speaker/ Interview	Example
7. Third Singular -s Absence	Leticia/0730d	Leticia: [oh, Jasmine.] Lalo: She 0 sayin she [**like**] me. Leticia: [I don't know cause—] maybe she **play** cause all—all boys in the [world **play.**]
8. Negative Concord	Celso (1808d)	Che: What else are we talking about? Are we still- are we still talking about that scary stuff? Int: Well, if you got any scary [stories,] yeah. Che: [<sniff>] Celso do. Celso: I **don't** got **none**.
9. Voiced th-stopping	Tony/dps 1050	Tony: I don't know if he's good at language arts. . . I don't know. And stuff like [**d**]at.
10. Presentational 'it' (for 'there + is/are)	Che/ dps1080d	Che: [describing experience at Wet 'n' Wild water theme park]: And. . . **it** was these bumper boats Int: Uh-[huh] Che: [I] got on.
11. 0 Possessive Marker	Tony/1050	Tony: I went to **aunt 0 house**—I mean, to my **uncle 0 house**.

course of transcribing and coding the data. Thus, there was not a focus on the unmarked tense variable; the goal was simply to document examples of AAE structures when they occurred to offer supportive data for the contact influence from this variety. The list is based on the canonical inventories of AAE features found in works such as Labov et al. (1968), Fasold and Wolfram (1970), Rickford (1999) and Green (2002), among others.

The speakers who appear in Table 4.3 represent a cross-section of speakers in the study: Lalo and Goyo, for example, are both 13-year-old gang-affiliated students at Rogers-Herr Middle School. Lalo is of Salvadoran descent, was born in Los Angeles and moved to Durham when he was 8-years old. Goyo arrived in the US from Mexico when he was 7. Luisa, by contrast, is a 9-year-old 4th grader who attends E.K. Powe (no gang affiliations were reported for any of the elementary school students). She was born in Mexico, learned to read in Spanish and came to the US when she was 7. She listens to pop music and has a European American best friend, Alex, with whom she speaks only English. Fely also attends E.K. Powe. She is an 8-year-old 3rd grader who arrived from Mexico before she started kindergarten and learned to read in English. Che is a 12-year-old non-gang-affiliated Chewning student from Morélia, Mexico, who came to the US even younger, when he was 2-years old, and learned to read in English.

Several of these features may not originate exclusively in AAE; a case could be made that at least some have their origins in Southern White Vernacular English (e.g., 3., 4., 8. and 9.). The relationship between African American and white varieties of English in the South is far from straightforward, as variation may show both superficial convergence, functional divergence, quantitative vs. qualitative differences and bilateral contact (AAE—>SWVE as well as SWVE—>AAE). The evidence presented in Table 4.3, however, demonstrates that key forms do pattern structurally and functionally with AAE, and several of them (e.g., habitual *be*, 0 possessive, etc.) are unique to AAE among American English language varieties. For example, when SWVE shows copula deletion, it tends to occur with *are*; similarly, uninflected 'be' usually occurs in contexts of underlying *would*-deletion (and not with a distributive/habitual function).[11]

4.11.2   CCR in NCHE and AAE

After it was established that HE speakers have AAE contact features in their repertoires, both the study data (n = 665) and a smaller subsection of data collected from AAE speakers in the speech community (n = 166) were coded according to the procedures described in sections 2.8.2 and 4.2 (i.e., in additional to cluster/bimorphemic tokens like 'picked,' monomorphemic tokens like 'test' were coded for phonological environment and morphemic status).[12] The supplementary AAE data come from sociolinguistic interviews with seven African American English speakers, aged 12–13, three males and four females, who attended Chewning Middle School. These speakers attended classes with the HE speakers in the study with the exception of an ESL class which met one period a day. All the AAE speakers reported that they had lived in the Piedmont region of North Carolina (Durham, NC or Raleigh, NC) all their lives.

A GOLDVARB[13] run on the HE data found a significant effect (p < .05) for following phonological environment, morphemic status, gender and LOR in years. The results for the first three factors are shown in Table 4.4. The results for LOR are shown in Figure 4.15.

Table 4.4 demonstrates that increasing LOR inhibits overall reduction, though at the upper LORs (5+ years; n = 407) both phonological environment (χ^2 = 17.67; p < .01) and morphemic status (χ^2 = 13.360; p < .001) still show significant effects. This pattern may be compared to the phenomenon described in section 3.5, where speakers in Detroit differ in the overall rate at which the CCR rule was applied, but not in overall constraints (or constraint orders). Additionally, Table 4.4 shows that there is an overall tendency for males to apply the CCR process over females (at a factor weight of .55 > .42), which is notable since there was no gender effect for

Table 4.4 Factor weights for three CCR factor groups

Factor	Factor Weight
1. Phonological Environment	
a. _C	.52
b. _P	.61
c. _V	.33
2. Morphemic Status	
a. Bimorpheme	.54
b. Monomorpheme	.63
3. Gender	
a. Male	.55
b. Female	.42

Log likelihood = -359.255
p = 0.031
Input = 0.64

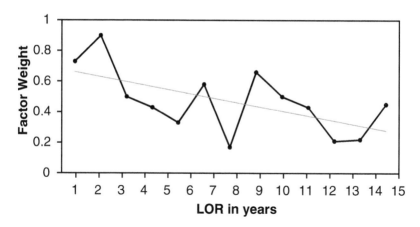

Figure 4.15 Factor weights for CCR by LOR

the grammatical variable of tense unmarking. This is evidence that the CCR variable may well have a social significance in the speech community that the grammatical effect of tense unmarking does not. The strands of this social significance may be more complicated to unravel here, however, since it is not clear 1) what particular social meaning CCR may have in this community nor 2) whether gender itself is a primary or secondary social index for this meaning (masculinity, for example, may well be linked to some third factor—school vs. community orientation, for example). More

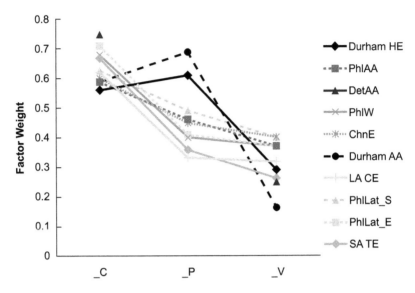

Figure 4.16 Factor weights for CCR by phonological environment for Durham HE
and nine English varieties

qualitative/ethnographic evidence would be needed to establish a precise social meaning for CCR in Durham HE.

Nevertheless, the linguistic constraints alone have important things to say about speakers' orientation to the community around them. Figure 4.16 and Figure 4.17 show both VARBRUL/GOLDVARB factor weights and raw percentages for CCR reduction for Durham HE and AAE as well as eight representative varieties of native and nonnative Englishes. These varieties include Detroit AAE (DetAA) (Wolfram 2003), Mexican American adolescent English in Gary, Indiana (GME) (Hartford 1975), Philadelphia AAE and European American English (PhlAA, PhlW) (Labov 2010), Los Angeles Chicano English (LA CE) (Santa Anna 1991), East Los Angeles (Wald 1981) and Chinese English interlanguage (ChnE) (Bayley 1991), San Antonio Tejano English (Bayley 1991) and Austin (TX) Chicano English (Galindo 1987).[14] The samples for Philadelphia come from the Urban Minorities Reading Project (UMRP) and include separate factor weights for Philadelphia Latinos who learned to read in Spanish (PhlLat_S) and English (PhlLat_).

There are several surprises in these findings. First, while showing the overall constraint ranking C > V, HE actually shows slightly higher rates

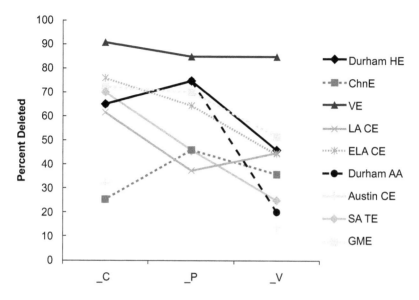

Figure 4.17 Percent CCR by phonological environment for Durham HE and six English varieties

for prepausal tokens (61%/75%), which usually pattern between _C and _V. The effect of pause, however, does show variation even in native speakers: for most of the native dialects of English analyzed by Guy (1980), a following P patterned with a following V; however for a few exceptions, it behaved like a following C. In terms of other Hispanicized English varieties, Hartford (1975), in a study of adolescent Mexican American speakers in Gary, Indiana, reports relatively high rates of CCR for prepausal tokens (70.1%) vs. prevocalic tokens (51.7%), with preconsonantal tokens still (narrowly) showing the highest rates of deletion (72.1%). Though Hartford coded only monomorphemic tokens to control for morphemic effect, it is interesting that another US Hispanicized English speech community shows CCR results where _C patterns with _P (with _V showing distinct effects).

Perhaps the more surprising finding is the similarities between the Durham HE constraints and the Durham AAE constraints, which mirror each other (factor weights .56/.62/.29 for HE and .59/.46/.37) in terms of the novel rank orders P > C > V. This same effect is found for Bayley's (1991) study of Chinese interlanguage, where, in terms of raw percentages, P > C > V (clusters are slightly less likely to be deleted before pauses than before vowels). Thus, there is limited evidence (the AAE sample used

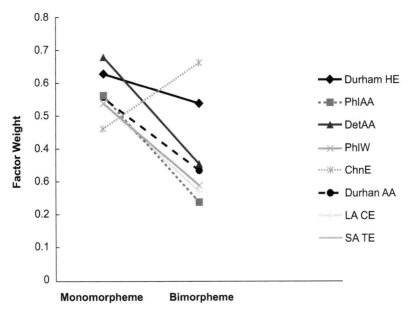

Figure 4.18 Factor weights by morphemic status for CCR for Durham HE and six
English varieties

here only consisted of seven speakers and 155 tokens) that HE speakers
in Durham do show convergence with native vernaculars in terms of the
phonological environment constraint on CCR. Furthermore, this result
is surprising since both HE and native varieties of AAE show the same
(idiosyncratic) rank ordering of constraints.

The results for grammatical category (shown in Figure 4.18 and
Figure 4.19) provide perhaps even more compelling evidence of HE
speakers' accommodation to the groups around them.

While the phonological constraints shown in Figure 4.13 and Figure 4.14
can be attributed to universal effects of articulatory factors, speakers must
ostensibly be attuned to finer, English-specific details around them to acquire
the morphosyntactic/grammatical constraint. Though the Durham HE
speakers do not show the great overall differences in the contrasting rates of
CCR for monomorphemes vs. bimorphemes that speakers of native English
vernaculars show (including English-dominant LA Chicano speakers), the
results in Figures 4.16–4.17 demonstrate that HE speakers are showing the
same speech norms as their (AAE-speaking) peers for this variable.

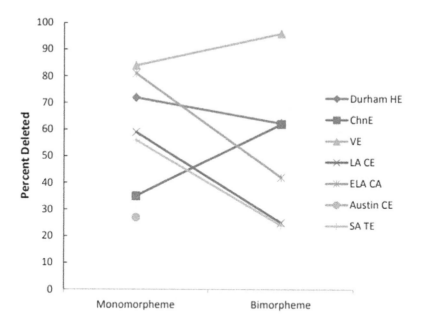

Figure 4.19 Percent CCR by morphemic status for Durham HE and five English
varieties

Interestingly, Durham speakers contrast with Labov's (2010) Latino
speakers in Philadelphia: neither UMRP group of 8–11-year-old children
(n = 397), those who learned to read in English nor those who learned to
read in Spanish, showed significant effects in terms of CCR for grammatical
status. Furthermore, the Spanish group did not show a significant effect for
the phonological constraint. In this context, Durham HE speakers show evidence of accommodation to local dialect traits whereas other interlanguage
varieties, including Vietnamese English and Chinese English, do not.

These results are further supported by the evidence presented in this chapter on tense unmarking, which demonstrates Durham speakers are expe-
riencing a steady retreat of the unmarking variable (see Figure 4.12); for
example, 61% for LOR 1 vs. 31% for LOR 15. The additive effect, where
learners are more likely to reduce an inflectional vs. lexical cluster due to
an additive effect of the grammatical and phonological processes (variable unmarking + variable CCR) does not operate in the same way in this
community as both Chinese English interlanguage and Vietnamese English
interlanguage (parallel lines in Figure 4.16). In this way, the Durham HE

community demonstrates it is sociolinguistically distinct from English Language Learner communities of speakers from both Chinese and Vietnamese backgrounds, as well as showing accommodation to local vernaculars in ways that other Latino communities do not.

4.11.3   Collinearity in Morphemic Status and Phonological Environment

After presenting the results for CCR for Durham HE and Durham HE using raw percentages and GOLDVARB figures, a logistic regression was used to analyze the CCR data in terms of the factors morphological status, phonological environment, LOR and gender—the factors GOLDVARB selected as significant). Surprisingly, the regression results showed a nonsignificant result was returned for morphemic status and gender, leaving only two factors to correlate significantly with CCR variation: phonological environment ($p < .000$) and LOR ($p < .05$). Further investigation revealed that an interaction effect contributed to the nonsignificant result: in fact, phonological environment and morphemic status are themselves correlated, both in Durham HE and in Durham AAE. In both the AAVE and HE CCR data, monomorphemes are more frequent than bimorphemes; in the same way, preconsonantal tokens themselves are more frequent than prepausal tokens, which are more frequent than prevocalic tokens (Figure 4.20):

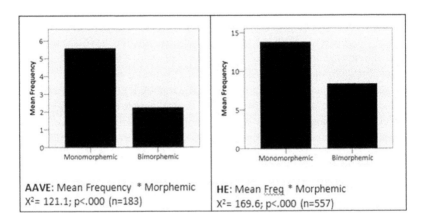

AAVE: Mean Frequency * Morphemic
$X^2 = 121.1$; $p<.000$ (n=183)

HE: Mean Freq * Morphemic
$X^2 = 169.6$; $p<.000$ (n=557)

Figure 4.20 Mean frequency for all tokens (marked and unmarked) by morphemic status and phonological environment: Durham AAVE and Durham HE

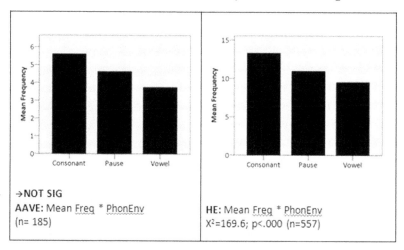

AAVE: Mean Freq * PhonEnv
(n= 185)

HE: Mean Freq * PhonEnv
X²=169.6; p<.000 (n=557)

Figure 4.20 (Continued)

We have observed the central effect of frequency on the unmarked tense vari-able in earlier sections, for lexical aspect and verb type/phonetic saliency, with an interaction for verb class/salience and frequency as well as stative type tokens and frequency. Furthermore, we established a frequency constraint for background/copula tokens. Figure 4.20 is a striking result since both CCR pat-terns themselves and the parallel results for CCR in both communities can be accounted for by token type (mono > bi; _C > _P > _V). An important caveat is that due to low total tokens in the AAE comparison data (n = 185 vs. n = 557 for HE), the results do not reach statistical significance for phonologi-cal environment; however, the descriptive results display the mirroring of the categories themselves. Thus for both AAE and HE, speakers use significantly *more* monomorphemes than bimorphemes in their speech overall (e.g., more one-morpheme words like *hand* than two-morpheme verbs with a past tense ending like *picked*); both communities of speakers also use cluster-final words more often *overall* before consonants in their discourse (more phrases like *picked through* than *picked up*).

The use of inference trees establishes that the most important factor for CCR in HE, with all factors included (phonological environment, aspect, morphemic status, school, gender, age, LOR) is phonological context, such that vowels pattern separately from consonants and pauses. For preconso-nantal and prepausal tokens, older speakers are *less* likely to use marked forms; for prevocalic tokens, speakers with longer LORs are *more* likely to use marked forms (Figure 4.21).

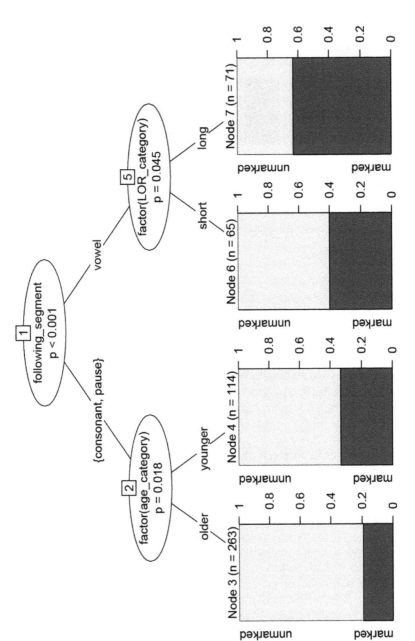

Figure 4.21 Inference tree for Durham HE CCR

These results call into question the older CCR studies (sections 3.3–3.4), which assume the structural independence of morphemic status and phonological environment and emphasize the importance of considering collinearity among factors when analyzing CCR.

4.12 Discussion: Past Tense Unmarking as Dialect Formation

Section 1.3 discussed several current models for new dialect formation in the context of language contact and acquisition, including Trudgill (1986), Thomason (2001) and Schneider (2003). One overarching thread in these accounts was the mechanism for rule formation: how do new dialect rules form in the first place? Language learners, interacting with and accommodating to structures in the target variety/L2, both remember widespread patterns from their native language and notice new patterns in the (frequent) pronunciations of words around them. There are, of course, also generalized interlanguage strategies that exploit regularities in the system—learning obvious things from obvious, overlapping cues.[15] In this section, I will attempt to bring together the threads of dialect formation processes in Durham in terms of both the quantitative results and the theoretical models previously named in order to document how past tense unmarking (via CCR) might have emerged in the Durham speech community. Specifically, I will rely on the following observations:[16]

1. In the early stages of contact and L2 acquisition, a structural 'founder effect' (Mufwene 1996, 2001) plays a central role as forms from the L1 and L2 compete in a pool of possible variants (Schneider 2003:[17] 240–241; Thomason 2001: 78–79). Even after generations of coexistence, some 'core' L1 features may contribute to a durable substrate effect in ethnically associated varieties of English (Wolfram 2003).

2. During a subsequent stage of EXNORMATIZE STABILIZATION (Schneider 2003: 246–249), bilingualism spreads and multilingualism is established. Here, speakers negotiate their forms to approximate what they believe to be (both phonological and structural) patterns of another language or dialect in their emerging speech community.

3. Grammatical features emerge as idiosyncratic usage patterns and complementation patterns develop into innovative rules; these lexico-grammatical constraints (Biber et al. 1999) help open up new structural possibilities that may ultimately modify the grammatical makeup of the (new) L2 (Schneider: 249).

4. As learners import features of the native language, highly integrated (embedded and intertwined L1 features) are most likely to survive

contact; in a complex type of interference, L1 structures may be projected onto systematic forms in the L2, as with the development of
the 'second genitive' in Standard Russian masculine noun cases (see
Figure 1.1) (Thomason 2001: 147).

5. Through largely automatic processes of accommodation (Giles 1973;
   Giles et al. 1973), as speakers come into contact with and talk to others
   in particular settings, structural processes produce linguistic changes in
   the emerging dialect (Trudgill 1986).

6. Phonological changes diffuse through the linguistic system on a word-by-
   word basis; as learners notice pronunciation patterns in particular words,
   they hypothesize that these patterns represent a general rule (Chambers
   1992: 693–695). In other words, phonological rules are actuated via phonetic accommodation to particular words in the speech community.

Here, linking 5. and 6. (rule actuation via phonetic accommodation by individuals) to the (co-)collinearity effect we have observed in terms of morphemic status and phonological environment in both Durham AAE and NCHE
(Figure 4.17) is a move that allows us to provide an articulated picture of
the mechanics of ethnolect emergence in terms of the NCHE unmarking
variable. Specifically, I will argue that it is possible to provide a precise
empirical account where accommodation is happening not via social means
as such (i.e., via agentive/identity-driven stances or orientations), but,
instead, socio-phonologically in the context of the local lexicon. I propose
that the frequencies of token types in the local input (e.g., more monomorphemes than bimorphemes and more cluster-final words before consonants
in discourse)—termed 'lexical bundles' by Biber et al. (1999)—constitute
the 'speech community' to which Durham NCHE and AAE speakers commonly belong. It is the sociophonological air around them—the patterns
of words and phrases they hear every day. The 'negotiation' described
in 2. occurs as language learners, very simply, listen to, understand and
generalize the sound structures frequently in everyday speech: this is language socialization via (local) statisticization. Having already established
the central effect of frequency on L2 learning patterns—both highly frequent tokens themselves (e.g., *be*) are almost categorically marked, even
by speakers at low LOR levels, and high frequency itself is simultaneously
characterized by high phonetic salience—makes the statistical-sociophono-
logical account even more attractive. It is at this point that grammatical
innovations (via 3. and 4.) come into play via lexico-grammatical effects.
We will recall that the lexical (inherent) aspect significantly affects marking
patterns in NCHE: telic accomplishments and achievements are marked at
higher rates than atelic achievements and non-copula states. This effect is
illustrated in discourse environments where past tense marking is highly
favored (e.g., narrative backgrounds) and high-frequency copula tokens are

used at significant rates. It should be no surprise that the Spanish aspectual system, which distinguishes between imperfective meanings (concomitant with atelic predicates) and perfective meanings (concomitant with telic predicates) are re-articulated on the basis of these lexico-grammatical cues. Here, distinctions that are discernable to Spanish L1 learners in terms of their native tense/aspect system drive a contact-based rule formation process much like the 'second genitive' effect proposed by Thomason (2001). Here, I provide a graph that may be compared with Thomason's account described in Chapter 1/Figure 1.1 (Figure 4.22):

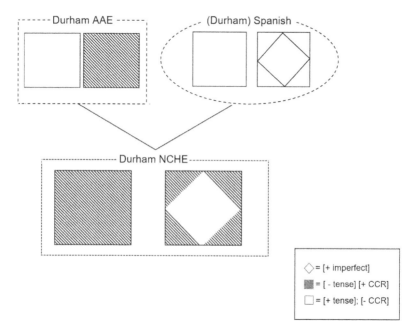

Figure 4.22 Development of Durham NCHE unmarked past tense

Elsewhere (Callahan 2008), I have argued for the unitary influence of two morphosyntactic constraints—(a) the effects of verb class and (b) a grammatical process of past tense unmarking—in the CCR patterns of two communities, both in Durham and in a longstanding, Chicano English-speaking community in south Texas. In both communities, unmarked tense patterns correlate significantly with Spanish imperfective function. The first constraint, (a), illustrates the potentially universal effect of phonetic salience in terms of verb class (e.g., regular vs. irregular; suppletive vs. replacive final consonant). The second, (b), illustrates the impact of the FOUNDER EFFECT (1.), where patterns from the native language (especially highly embedded functions like those described in 4.) survive contact and are preserved in ethnically aligned varieties of the emerging variety. These durable substrate effects occur in both Spanish L1 communities (south Texas and Durham), as with AAE speakers in disparate NC enclave communities (Wolfram 2003), even after multiple generations.[18]

In sum, unmarked tense, as a grammatical structure that is reinforced in the sociophonological input, illustrates a linguistically coherent process of EXNORMATIZE STABILIZATION (2.). Crucially, the structural/linguistic factors, all tightly inter-related, are at the forefront of the process of change and development; we need not, at this point, rely on identity-driven forces; speakers can simply 'lean on the lexicon.' Trudgill (2008: 252), arguing against the role of identity in the initial developmental of colonial varieties of European languages, concludes that new dialect formation in these settings may be more "mechanical and inevitable" than socially driven, the result of relatively automatic processes of personal interaction and linguistic diffusion. Similarly, Wolfram and Myrick (2015), describing variation in ethnically associated varieties in the Afro-English diaspora, emphasize the role of individual language contact, robust founder effects and substrate sustainability (e.g. null copula) over agentive change in accounting for the genesis and development of these new varieties—while allowing for structural differences to become emblematic across ethnolinguistic boundaries in the context of sociohistorical and interactional changes (e.g., post-WWII integration). In this embryonic stage, NCHE may, like other ethnically associated forms derived from Spanish-English contact in the US, be unfolding structurally in relatively automatic ways that become socially salient in the fullness of time, space and local contexts of interaction.

In all, the Durham speakers provide striking evidence for how ethnolect grammars develop by sourcing both idiosyncratic norms present in English interlanguage as well as the local grammars of a speech community of peers. They demonstrate that second-language learning and second dialect configuration cannot be thought of as two separate processes. As an ethnolect stabilizes, its speakers incorporate both nonnative (aspectual marking) and native English rules (marking by phonological environment), and these rules continue to operate even for speakers who know very little Spanish. In this way, the Durham speakers provide vivid empirical evidence of language change in terms of language learning, language contact and ethnolect emergence as speakers configure their own norms while simultaneously incorporating local patterns.

4.13   Summary of Results

In sum, emerging Hispanic English in Durham, NC shows a complex array of internal/linguistic, discourse-based and social constraints that not only reliably constrain past tense marking patterns, but also constrain each other as part of a unitary, context-driven process of language learning. In large part, the same kinds of linguistic constraints and constraint hierarchies demonstrated for previous studies of English interlanguage, including Wolfram's (2003) study of Vietnamese English and Bayley's (1991) studies of Chinese English, are reflected in the Durham Hispanic English data.

Taken together, this cohort of variationist studies of English interlanguage confirm the central influence of verb class on unmarking patterns in terms of a hierarchy of phonetic saliency, where tokens that are highly phonetically differentiated to learners (*go* vs. *went*) are marked at higher rates over tokens that are not as phonetically distinct in terms of segments shared with a stem ('learn' vs. 'learned'). The verb class constraint is reliably articulated by LOR and frequency with the exception of copula tokens, which interact in meaningful ways with the verbal predicate state, the verb class suppletive and the frequency constraint. Here, the data show that high frequency is simultaneously phonetically salient: the two effects cannot be divorced since they mutually support each other and, in turn, the process of language learning, which is largely driven by redundancy. The most perceptually salient tokens (irregulars) can only afford to occur at high frequencies to resist leveling by generalization, a process that has been spelled out over the long haul by historical change in English (strong to weak preterit drift). In turn, learners reach for these familiar, distinct forms to structure their discourse in terms of low-risk, high-reward strategies like exploiting copula to fill in the background of a narrative in order to 'set the stage' for optionally marked foregrounded events. Thus, on the one hand, in future studies, care should be taken to allow for the effects of super high-frequency tokens like 'be' and 'go,' which may skew the results of a traditional, variationist analysis (i.e., if factor groups are not specified at the word level). On the other hand, in the context of an evidence-rich learning environment, learners may well be exploiting the synergistic effect exhibited by highly frequent tokens that are simultaneously highly phonetically salient.

Notes

1. Erker and Guy (2012), in a study of variable subject personal pronoun (SPP) frequency in Puerto Rican Spanish, found that frequency was best coded as a discrete vs. continuous variable since it acted as 'gatekeeper' on stable patterns of variation in other factors. Common verbs that occurred above a certain frequency (e.g., *creer* 'to believe,' *saber* 'to know' and *ver* 'to see') seemed to amplify the effects of other factors like person and number. Below a certain threshold, however, these effects rapidly diminished (person and number showed no significant effect on SPP patterns for verbs *amenezar* 'to threaten' or *convivir* 'to exist'). We will return to a discussion of frequency in Durham HE later in this chapter.

2. LOR has been considered an epiphenomenon for various other factors, including proficiency and cultural assimilation.

3. The -2 log likelihood is similar to an F-test in linear regression.

4. Though acquisition is assumed to differ in qualitative terms across learning environments (e.g., naturalistic acquisition in the L2 speech community vs. formal instruction/classroom learning), we might also speculate that more or less attention to speech could outline the same trajectory as acquisition over time.

5. Bayley (personal communication) reports that the relatively low rate of copula marking in his Chinese English data may be indicative of an L1 effect since copula is widely nonobligatory in Chinese: among lower proficiency learners, he found copula could be absent while, among higher proficiency learners, copula could be present but not marked.

6. The effects of stress may be relevant as well; for example, internal vowel change tokens may share relatively more segments than weak syllabics; however, the vowel in IVC forms is always stressed (*be'come—> be'came*) whereas the *-ed* form never is (*want—> wanted*).

7. Pauses of more than approximately one second are annotated (.); pauses of a second or less are annotated with—.

8. All confidence intervals were set to 95%. For continuous variables (LOR, age), correlations are in terms of Pearson r in terms of a paired-samples t-test.

9. Interestingly, when the phonological process is included in the model (i.e., accounting not only for the results of bimorphemic/verbal tokens like 'pick' but monomorphemic tokens like 'test'), the relationship between reduction (whether verbal or not) and the following social variables *does* reach significant levels: age ($p < .01$), interview ($p < .01$) and, almost, country of birth ($p = .051$). Especially in light of the dependency between LOR and those social variables and the lower indices of significance within this model (i.e., more room for chance), this effect is not discussed here.

10. For comprehensive features lists for AAE, see Green (2002).This source was also used as reference in compiling Table 4.3.

11. Consult Wolfram (1974), Fasold et al. (1987) and Bailey (2001) for further reading on Black and white speech differences in the South.

12. Only clusters that ended in a stop and shared voicing were coded, e.g., [st] but not [nt]. Derivational tokens (*slept, told*) were not considered since they were originally coded as marked for tense if they showed a vowel change with cluster reduction (i.e., [slɛp] and [slɛpt] were both coded as marked but not [slip]).

13. GOLDVARB is an updated version of the VARBRUL program described in Chapter 2.

14. Where following C was articulated into subgroups (e.g., obstruent, liquid, glide, etc.), the figures for obstruent were used in the graphs. This convention was followed for data from Bayley (1991) and Labov (2010).

15. In the Durham data, this principle becomes visible as learners mark high-frequency tokens, led by suppletives like *go—>went* at consistently higher rates; the characteristics of these highly frequent token types are they are highly phonetically distinct/have increased lexical strength (Bybee 2001).

16. Though the processes described in 1.–5. are listed in rough chronological order, they are not meant to be seen as strictly sequential; I propose only that they function together at relevant stages of the contact/acquisition process.

17. Note that Schneider's stages are 'macro' categories—referring to broad social trends—while Thomason (2001) refers to individual-level 'micro' categories/processes.

18. I offer a few caveats. I am not adopting (nor attempting to excude) either a neo-grammarian-type regular theory of sound change (e.g. Labov 1994) nor a lexical diffusion approach (e.g. Chen & Wang 1975). Instead, in 1-.6., I assemble observations which inform an empirical, descriptive account of the emergence and development of contact and ethnically-associated varieties of English (i.e. in terms of NCHE). At the beginning and end of language change, lexical elements are highly prominent; this is one form of lexical diffusion, where learners notice and use the word forms around them. Second, I draw upon both indivdual-level, 'mirco'-type elements of Thomason's (2001) model as well as societal-level, 'macro'-elements of Schneider (2003). Again, I note these simultaneous (and perhaps complementary) phenomena in order to provide descriptive account of language contact and the early emergence of an ethnically-associated variety of English, NCHE.

References

Adamson, H. D. 2009. *Interlanguage variation in theoretical and pedagogical perspective*. New York: Routledge.

Bailey, G. 2001. The relationship between African American and white vernaculars in the American South: A sociocultural history and some phonological evidence. In Lanehart, S. (ed.), *Sociocultural and Historical Contexts of African American English*. Philadelphia: John Benjamins.

Bayley, R. J. 1991. *Variation theory and second language learning: Linguistic and social constraints on interlanguage tense marking*. Unpublished doctoral dissertation. Stanford University, Stanford, CA.

Biber, D., S. Johansson, G. Leech, S. Conrad, and E. Finegan. 1999. *Longman grammar of spoken and written English*. Harlow: Longman.

Brown, E. L., and R. T. Cacoullos. 2002. *¿Qué le vamoh aher?*: Taking the syllable out of Spanish /s/-reduction. *University of Pennsylvania Working Papers in Linguistics* (Papers from NWAV 30) 8.3.17–31.

Bybee, J. L. 2001. *Phonology and language use*. Cambridge: Cambridge University Press.

Callahan, E. E. 2008. *Accommodation without assimilation: Past tense unmarking and peak accent alignment in Hispanic English*. Master's Thesis. North Carolina State University. Retrieved from NCSU Digital Repository <http://repository.lib.ncsu.edu/ir/bitstream/1840.16/2085/1/etd.pdf> on 10/1/2012.

Carter, P. M. 2014. National narratives, institutional ideologies, and local talk: The discursive production of Spanish in a 'new' U.S. Latino community. *Language in Society 43*.2: 209–240.

Chambers, J. K. 1992. Dialect acquisition. *Language 68.4*: 673–705.

Clark, L., and K. Watson. 2011. Testing claims of a usage-based phonology with Liverpool English t-to-r. *English Language and Linguistics 15.3*: 523–547.

Ellis, R. 1987. Interlanguage variability in narrative discourse: Style shifting in the use of the past tense. *Studies in Second Language Acquisition 9*: 1–20.

Erker, D., and G. Guy. 2012. The role of lexical frequency in syntactic variability: Variable subject personal pronoun expression in Spanish. *Language 88.3*: 526–557.

Fasold, R. W., Labov, W., Vaughn-Cooke, F. B., Bailey, G., Wolfram, W., Spears, A. K. and J. Rickford. 1987. Are Black and White Vernaculars Diverging? Papers from the NWAVE XIV Panel Discussion. *American Speech 62:1*: 3–80.

Fasold, R., and W. Wolfram. 1970. Some linguistic features of Negro dialect. In Fasold, R. and R. Shuy (eds.), *Teaching standard English in the inner city*: 41–86. Washington, DC: Center for Applied Linguistics.

Galindo, D. L. 1987. Linguistic influence and variation on the English of Chicano Adolescents in Austin, Texas. Doctoral dissertation. University of Texas at Austin. Austin, TX.

Giles, H. 1973. Accent mobility: A model and some data. *Anthropological Linguistics 15*: 87–105.

Giles, H., D. Taylor, and R. Bourhis. 1973. Towards a theory of interpersonal accommodation through speech: Some Canadian data. *Language in Society 2*: 177–192.

Green, L. 2002. *African American English: A linguistic introduction.* Cambridge: Cambridge University Press.

Hartford, B. A. S. 1975. *The English of Mexican American adolescents in Gary, Indiana: A sociolinguistic description.* Doctoral dissertation. University of Texas at Austin, Austin, TX.

Kumpf, L. 1984. Temporal systems and universality in interlanguage: A case study. In Eckman, F., L. Bell and D. Nelson (eds.), *Universals of second language acquisition*: 132–143. Rowley, MA: Newbury House.

Labov, W. 2010. The diffusion of language from group to group. In Labov, W. (ed.), *Principles of linguistic change* (vol. 3). Oxford: Wiley-Blackwell.

Labov, W., P. Cohen, C. Robins, and J. Lewis. 1968. *A study of the nonstandard English of Negro and Puerto Rican speakers in New York City.* Final Report, Cooperative Research Project No. 3288. United States Office of Education.

Mufwene, S. S. 1996. The founder principle in creole genesis. *Diachronica 13*: 83–134.

Mufwene, S. S. 2001. *The ecology of language evolution.* Cambridge: Cambridge University Press.

Poplack, S. 2001. Variability, frequency and productivity in the irrealis domain of French. In Bybee, J. & P. Hopper (eds.), *Frequency and the Emergence of Linguistic Structure*: 405–428. Amsterdam: Benjamins.

Pray, L. 2005. How well do commonly used language instruments measure English oral-language proficiency? *Bilingual Research Journal 29.2*: 387–409.

Rickford, J. 1999. *African American English: Features, evolution, educational implications.* Malden, MA: Blackwell.

Rubin, D. L. 1992. Nonlanguage factors affecting undergraduate's judgments of nonnative English-speaking teaching assistants. *Research in Higher Education 33*: 511–531.

Santa Ana, O. 1991. Phonetic simplification processes in the English of the barrio: A cross- generational sociolinguistic study of the Chicanos of Los Angeles. Doctoral dissertation. University of Pennsylvania, Philadelphia, PA.

Schneider, E. 2003. The dynamics of New Englishes: From identity construction to dialect birth. *Language 79*: 233–281.

Shirai, Y., and R. W. Andersen. 1995. The acquisition of tense-aspect morphology: A prototype account. *Language 71.4*: 743–62.

Spears, Arthur K. 1982. The Black English Semi-Auxiliary *come. Language 58*: 850–72.

Thomason, S. G. 2001. *Language contact: An introduction.* Washington, DC: Georgetown University Press.

Trudgill, P. 1986. *Dialects in contact.* Oxford: Basil Blackwell.

Trudgill, T. 2008. Colonial dialect contact in the history of European languages: On the irrelevance of identity to new-dialect formation. *Language in Society 37*: 241–280.

Wald, B. 1981. The status of Chicano English as a dialect of American English. In Ornstein-Galicia, J. (ed.), *Form and Function in Chicano English.* Rowley, MA: Newbury House.

Wolfram, W. 1974. The relationship of white southern speech to vernacular Black English. *Language 50.3*: 498–527.

Wolfram, W. 2003. Reexamining the development of African American English: Evidence from isolated communities. *Language 79.2*: 282–316.

Wolfram, W., and D. Hatfield. 1984. *Tense marking in second language learning: Patterns of spoken and written English in a Vietnamese community.* Washington, DC: Center for Applied Linguistics.

Wolfram, W. and C. Myrick. 2015. Linguistic commonality in English of the African Diaspora: Evidence from lesser-known varieties of English. In Cutler, C., Vrzic, Z., and P. Angemeyer (eds.), *Language contact in Africa and the African Diaspora in the Americas.* Philadelphia/Amsterdam: John Benjamins.

5 Pedagogical Perspectives
Ethnolects Go to School

INT 1: *Have you- have you always been in ESL classes?*
Lori: *Well, I- I don't know, but . . .*
INT 1: *As long as you can remember.*
Lori: *But, my mom say then when- when I was born here, I did not went to ESL classes, like that. But when I came back [from* el D. F. *[Mexico City]], I forgot everything of English.*
INT 1: *Do you speak to your parents in English or Spanish?*
Lori: *Both.*
INT 2: *Does it depend?*
Lori: *Yeah, it depends.*
INT 1: *On what you're talking about?*
Lori: *Uh-huh.*
INT 1: *When do you. speak in Spanish with them?*
Lori: *Well, I speak more Spanish than English in my house . . . it's like, we have like, when we talk or something like that, we talk in Spanish. Or when we playing around, something like that, we talk in English.*
INT 1: *When you're playing around?*
Lori: *With my cousin and- yeah.*
INT: *Oh, okay. Your cousin that speaks as much English as you, or not as much?*
Lori: *Well, he use—well, we speak the same English but . . . like, he pass the ESL test.*
INT 1: *Uh-huh.*
Lori: *Yeah. So he's not in ESL.*

5.1 Preliminaries: We Are All (Socio)Linguistic Geniuses

If there's one thing I want you to remember after this class, I tell the teacher candidates in my English education and Teaching English as a Second Language (TESOL) courses, it's this: *we are all linguistic geniuses*. The amount of information processed in your brain—not just sounds, but what drastically different meanings tiny differences can produce (differences that may be invisible to nonnative speakers) and how your tongue and lips produce these sounds in precise combinations (and what other sounds can come before, after or not at all); not just grammar but what other elements of the sentence must also occur, have occurred (or may not occur); not just pitch but at what point in a syllable to be slightly louder and how to time that syllable with respect to all other syllables (all decisions made in milliseconds)—all this information, I tell them, when crunched simultaneously, would crash the Pentagon's largest supercomputer. This is before we start coding for social significance: *did her vowel in 'pin' sound the same as the one in 'pen'?—she must be from the South; did he just pronounce that l-sound at the end of the word 'little' the same way as the sound at the beginning?—he must speak Spanish; did she blink her eyes? Did he sigh? Sniff? Turn over his palm? Shrug his shoulder?* Then I ask the class a question: do you think you do all this in another language—perfectly—and perhaps hundreds of times every few seconds? *That is what we ask language learners to do:* when they are 12-, 8-, or 4-years old. Every hour, day and month of their lives while they are in school.

The corollary to this statement is this, I tell the class: every dialect does all these things equally with regard to any other. They all have rules; the rules are just different, the way French and Russian are different. The reason we call one language a 'dialect' and one a 'language' has nothing to do with the linguistic forms speakers use (how logical, complex or consistent they are)—it has everything to do with what we think of the speakers themselves. The fact that all human language varieties are equal in linguistic terms is entirely uncontroversial for linguists (*Linguistic Society of America 1997*). It is ferociously, perniciously controversial in all other facets of day-to-day life.

For linguists, a dialect is simply any given language variety that is shared by a group of speakers (e.g., region, social class, ethnicity or age). Dialects may differ in terms of their sounds (pronouncing the vowels in *pen* and *pin* the same way, or not pronouncing the *r* at the end of the word *father*), their words (*yard* sale vs. *garage* sale; *y'all* vs. *youse guys* vs. *you all*) and their grammar (*He made money a-fishin'* in Appalachian English, or *She don't usually be there* in African American English (AAE)). No dialect or language is more 'correct' than any other: all human languages are equally rule governed: for instance, just as it would be incorrect in Spanish to say *el niño tuvo dos años* instead of *el niño tenía dos años* (i.e., the Spanish imperfect is used to talk about age and general conditions in the past, not the preterit), it would be incorrect to say *He a-fished that stream at 2pm* in Appalachian English or *She be busy right now* in AAE. In other words, dialect speakers don't try and fail to produce sentences of Standard English—they succeed at following the unique rules of their own system.

Any physical or social separation can produce dialects. For instance, a region's settlement history, immigration or natural barriers like mountains or rivers can create isolation from the home country/language as well as from local populations. In addition, factors like class, status and power differences or historical segregation patterns can create social distance, inhibiting the interaction of groups over time. Finally, natural changes in language patterns can cause one strand of language development to veer off into several directions, much like the branches of a family tree. This kind of language change is natural and inevitable: we don't speak Shakespearean English, and it works fine for our time and place. Though older generations, for example, may rail against the 'corrosion' or 'degradation' of Standard English, language is always in state of evolution, and there's little we can do to stop it. Differences that we take for granted now as entirely uncontroversial had periods of time when they were so wrong-sounding as to invite ridicule. My students are often surprised to hear that the word *apron*, in older forms of English, used to be *napron*; when English speakers in the past heard the phrase *a napron*, they simply segmented it incorrectly (*a napron—> an apron*). The older *napron* form is preserved in words with similar meaning, for instance, *napkin* in English, *nappe* ('tablecloth') in French. Along these lines, when I hear my students say *I'm so excited for Spring Break*—despite the fact that I too am excited—the sentence still sounds very wrong. I might say *I'm excited for Tasha; she's getting married*, meaning I am excited on Tasha's behalf (she is a living, breathing human being). When I hear my students talk, some part of my mind thinks "Why are they excited on behalf of a holiday?"

5.2   (Mis)Identification

Consider the following two statements:

> The transition into the Syntactic Stage occurs, and the child is now able to communicate more effectively with other speakers of the language. The child continues to expand his or her knowledge of vocabulary, and greater use of adjectives, adverbs, and prepositions, and verbal expressions is demonstrated. Admittedly, this use of language is primitive in nature, but further interaction with speakers of the language provides opportunities to experiment and refine personal skills.
>
> (Ballard et al. 1995: 2)

> Language differences as we see them are symbolic of cultural distance. They become instruments of educational failure when they are interpreted in a way to predict and insure this failure.
>
> Spears (1982), qtd. in Fasold et al. (1987)

These two passages represent very different perspectives on the nature of language differences in language-minority populations. The second excerpt comes from a special symposium of academic sociolinguists convened in the 1980s to address language change in African American English (AAE)-speaking populations—as well as the impact of this linguistic change on the educational experience of AAE-speaking children. The participants in this symposium are scientists: they view language differences (in terms of so-called language varieties or dialects) neutrally: their mission is to accurately *describe* language structure overall, not *prescribe* what language structure should be. Specifically, these sociolinguists study the nature of language variation in part to understand how language changes and why, as well as to uncover which social forces correlate with language change. One educational application of the field of sociolinguistics is to understand the implications of language differences/variation for the educational experience of dialect speakers in schools.

The first excerpt, by contrast, views language differences—here, the developing interlanguage of English Language Learners (ELLs)—in 'better or worse' terms. Early stages of language development are 'primitive,' representing language differences that must be eliminated, overcome or 'refined.' This excerpt comes from section 1.1 of *Examiner's manual of the IPT I: IDEA oral language proficiency test of English*, "Theoretical Considerations in Language Acquisition and Language Learning," the standardized test instrument I used as a K-12 ESL teacher in rural Granville County (NC) Schools from 2003 to 2005.[1] With a caseload of almost 100 students, teachers in the county schools were required to evaluate both new enrollees and students already receiving English as a Second Language (ESL) services twice a year in reading, writing and oral skills.

As a linguist, one of the first experiences I had as a new teacher was realizing that an appreciable number of monolingual speakers of local and regional dialects would be scored by the IPT Oral test as English Language Learners. Features like negative concord were evaluated as transfer features from Spanish ('I didn't do nothing' vs. Sp. *No hice nada*) for students who were monolingual in English—these patterns occurred not due to the influence of Spanish but because of the influence of nonstandard (L1) English.

I was curious how the Hispanicized English (HE) speakers in the study, especially those who were English dominant or English monolinguals, would fare on the IPT Oral test I had used. In order to address this question, I compiled skill items from the syntax strand of the IPT *Oral examiner's manual* (2007) and then matched these items with examples from the HE corpus, using both my own transcribed data as well as data transcribed by other graduate student fieldworkers in SLAAP (see section 4.3 and Kendall (2007)). Table 8 shows the skill items, taken from Forms A-B of this edition of the IPT-I Oral test (2007: 15, 23 (forms

Table 5.1 Oral IPT test by skill area (syntax) with HE examples

Skill Area	Speaker/Token
10. Yes/No Response	Tony (12y, LOR 5): *She told me '0 You tryin' to learn English?'* (dps1050d)
11. Regular Plurals	Cleo (13y, LOR 10 years): *I have **two sister** 0, and that's all.* (dps0050d)
12. Verb 'to be'	Paco (15y, LOR 6): *His name **0** Mr. Capone* (dps0030d)
17. Pronouns: Subject	Jackson 10y, LOR 8: ***Them** had a birthday party.* (dps052)
18. Verbs: Present Progressive	Lori (12y, LOR 10): *When we **0** playin' around, somethin' like that, we talk in English.* (dps0040d)
19. Mass Nouns	-
20. Conjunctions	-
21. Negative Statements	Graciela (13y, LOR 7):. . . *and when I woke up I didn't know **nothing*** (dps0800d)
33. Verbs: Habitual Present	Marcos (13y, LOR 10): *They **0** be like 'You go first,' and all that.* (dps0110)
35. Comparatives	Jorge (13y, LOR 13): ?*I'm more loved than them.* (dps0402d)
40. Questions: Future Tense	-
45. Irregular Plurals	-
46. Pronouns: Possessive	Luisa (9y, LOR 3): *We made this friendship bracelet, but I forgot **mines**.* (dps0280d)
53. Superlatives	-
54. Verbs: Irregular Past Tense	Fely (8y, LOR 4): *Then Fiona **think** that Shrek was in her room. . . .* (dps1271)

C-D duplicate the same skill items) as well as matched examples from the HE data.

Using only the sentences transcribed for unmarked tense/CCR as well as the few Durham HE interviews partially transcribed in SLAAP, I was able to fill in 10 of the 15 skill areas (67%) with nonstandard English examples that would be scored as errors by the IPT Oral test. To give some context, a 2nd grader who made nine or more errors in the context of both the syntax and other sections (verbal expression, e.g., retelling the main ideas of a story or vocabulary, naming animals on the farm) would be designated Non-English Speaking [NES] according to the test. A 6th grader who made four or more errors on this in conjunction with any other section of the test would be designated Limited English Speaking [LES].

Fought (2003) describes the same experience in the California high school where she was conducting ethnographic field work—and sometimes helped in the office:

> One of the things I was occasionally asked to do was to administer the Bilingual Syntax Measure, a test designed to help the school classify certain students as 'LEP' (Limited English Proficient). The test focuses on a number of English morphological forms, such as *-ed* for past tense, irregular verbs, plural *-s* and so on. The test was administered to any student whose parents had reported, in a survey sent home by the school, that Spanish was spoken at home. I dutifully administered the test and recorded the scores. Often, students who were completely fluent in English and fairly poor in Spanish were classified as LEP because of the non-standard forms they used in responding to the questions. . . . When I naively tried to convey all of this to the principal of the school, she looked at me with the expression that professionals in the 'real world' reserve for academics, and explained patiently that the money the government provided for LEP students was important to the school, and that the question of exactly why their English was low-scoring was somewhat irrelevant.
>
> (p. 4)

In my experience, many Hispanic(-looking) students were predestined for misidentification before they even entered the first day of elementary school. At initial enrollment, in addition to submitting birth certificates, vaccine reports and proof of residency in the county, parents were required to fill out a Home Language Survey (HLS) (NC Department of Public Instruction 2008), which asked the following questions:

1. What is the first language the student learned to speak?
2. What language does the student speak most often?
3. What language is most often spoken in the home?

A non-English response to any of these three questions ensured the student would be administered the IPT (state-identified English language proficiency test) within 30 days ("[i]f the answer to any question on the home language survey is "other than English," the student is considered a language-minority student (*Guidelines for testing students identified as limited English proficient*, NC Public Schools 2005: 15).[2] Carter (2014) observed an identical effect in the school norms of the NCHE (North Carolina Hispanicized English) site he researched, noting that many "native speakers of English are nevertheless assigned to ESL on the basis of surnames or presumed home language" (2014: 219). Thus, ELL (mis)identification was an unequivocal process: a non-English response on 1.–3. of the HLS flagged the student for IPT test administration, and the IPT identified the student as LEP. The student remained identified as LEP until s/he scored 'superior' on all subtests (listening, speaking, reading, writing) at the yearly administration of the IPT.[3]

For context, the English Proficiency Level Descriptions used in the NC Public Schools characterizes as 'intermediate high' a student who, in terms of speaking, "makes occasional errors in idiom and structure, often obscuring meaning" (NC Department of Public Instruction 2005: 40). Here, it is worth noting that, in only transcriptions of unmarked tense forms, I was able to locate 10 structures that would be characterized as 'errors' according to these descriptions. In the writing strand, the descriptor notes that intermediate-low students should be able to demonstrate "[e]vidence of good control of basic sentence construction and inflections such as subject/verb agreement; and straightforward syntactic constructions in present, past, and future time though errors occasionally occur" (NC Department of Public Instruction 2005: 39). Here, constructions such as omitted *be* verbs (Table 8/12.), omitted *be* auxiliaries (18.), negative concord (21.) and nonstandard present habitual constructions (33.) all qualify as sentences structures that indicate limited English proficiency. In terms of inflections, one NCHE-speaking student in this study who had been in the US for 8 years still showed over 50% unmarking of past tense verbs; another who had been in the US more than 15 years still unmarked a third of all past tense forms (Figure 4.22). These sentences are 'basic' to the descriptive NCHE grammar in that they are logical, rule-governed elements of the syntactic and phonological domains of a coherent system: the system happens to be an ethnically associated form of English (often the native system of speakers who know little or no Spanish). For reference, the full English Proficiency Level Descriptions for grades 3–12 are given in Appendix A.

Here, it is important to establish that even native (non-NCHE) monolingual speakers of English risk being labeled not proficient by the IPT. In a study of 40 native English-speaking, low, middle and upper SES elementary-aged speakers from 32 schools in one large urban city in the US, Pray (2005) found that a full 15% of students were classified by the IPT as non-English speaking (NES) or limited English speaking (12%).[4] In addition to the nonstandard English features used by NCHE and AAE speakers in this study, Pray notes that the IPT measures register academic/ institutional fluency in addition to language structures. For example, students are required to answer with a complete sentence when asked questions like, "Do you drive your teacher's car?" and, "What do you do during lunchtime after you eat?" Reponses like *No* and *Play on the playground* (instead of *No, I don't/do not* and *I play on the playground*) are judged as incomplete sentences. Finally, the IPT effectively measures memory as well as language proficiency: for example, in the story-retell phase of the test, the test examiner reads this passage to the students: "John is going to the airport with his parents. They are taking a trip to visit his grandmother who lives in the city. John and his parents will fly on a plane." Students are then asked, "Where does the grandmother live?" Here, it is the degree to which students can remember details, not language itself, which is being tested. I vividly remember reading this story to monolingual, elementary-aged English-speaking students who, despite speaking little Spanish, still called their grandmother *Abue* (from Spanish *Abuela* 'grandmother'), knew no one named John and had never seen an airplane.[5] As Pray puts it, "How can children who speak English as a second language be expected to perform well on tests that fail to measure native speaking ability of even native English-speaking children?" (2005: 405).

These specific issues are compounded by the systemic failures in norming and validity that plague standardized language tests in general. For example, standardized, paper-and-pencil tests such as the IPT often fail to assess language use in real-world communicative contexts like those described in the 2005 English Proficiency Level Descriptions (Geisinger and Carlson 1992; Hernández 1994) (Appendix A). Second, for bilingual (especially Spanish-dominant) students, English language tests like the IPT do not achieve the same content validity as tests in the native language (Figueroa 1990). Third, but certainly not last, is the fact that the language attitudes of test examiners may significantly influence comprehensibility ratings: NC IPT examiners (most often, ESL teachers) are told, for instance, that a speaking score of 'intermediate high' should only be assigned to a student who "[p]articipates *effectively* [my emphasis], sometimes hesitatingly, in social and academic conversations" (NC Department of Public Instruction 2005: 40) and whose errors do not obscure meaning. Here, the question of whose 'effectiveness' and whose 'obscuration' is significant, however—above and beyond the actual linguistic forms used, since the (often unconscious) ideologies of human examiners tends to, in some cases, be a self-fulfilling prophecy. Rubin (1992) designed an experiment to test comprehensibility ratings in the context of language attitudes about second-language speech. In this study, two groups of students listened to the same recorded lecture; one group was told that the professor was a native English speaker and the other group was told that the professor spoke English as a second language. Perhaps unsurprisingly, the second group reported more difficulty understanding the lecture and performed worse on a post-test measurement of understanding of the lecture's content. This analysis shows that meanings are more likely to be 'obscure[d]' if the speaker is judged to be a nonnative speaker at all. In a related way, teacher expectations of (language) minority students have been shown to correlate with students' lack of confidence on verbal tests (Labov 1972), negative psychological consequences for students, and a lack of test validity in demonstrating their intellectual abilities (Steele and Aronson 1995).

Finally, misidentification may not only have negative effects on students, but also far-reaching economic and institutional consequences. For example, North Carolina statewide funding for LEP students for the 2012–2013 budget was $84,463,502 (Matteson 2013). Thus, if even a 3% improvement were made in accurately identifying ELLs, the savings to the state system could be in the millions of dollars. Alternately, by maintaining current funding levels and effecting a 3% reduction in caseloads, ESL teacher-to-student ratios could be lowered, allowing for more contact hours of (higher quality) instruction and, ostensibly, earlier exit from the program for all students.

To sum up, this discussion in this section underlines of importance of linguistically informed accounts of ELL identification in multidialectal speech communities. In order to provide effective ESL services to students who have a genuine need, (monolingual) nonstandard English speakers first must be distinguished from English Language Learners. The first step in this process is a contextualized, accurate and linguistically informed account of the language ELLs actually have—as well as the native varieties of English of their peers. Since teachers (ESL but also content-area teachers, who see students most often) are often at the 'front lines' of this identification process, they can be the single most important factor in determining whether a student is accurately identified. Most school districts and program coordinators—and all parents—have legal guidelines for allowing some discretion in initial screening (NC Department of Public Instruction 2005: 15–16); ideally, the screening process should be one that is well informed by parents, administrators and teachers who are equipped with current findings on Second Language Acquisition and nonstandard varieties of English.

The most important purpose of state-mandated language proficiency tests is to protect the legal rights of linguistic minority students.[6] Therefore, it is critically important, above all, that every emerging bilingual student who needs ESL services receives them—indeed, school districts and teachers are legally obligated to ensure that this process takes place. However, with raised awareness, it need not be a process that excludes monolingual (nonstandard) English speakers from also receiving educational support that is individualized to their needs. On a personal note, my only regret after working as a K-12 ESL teacher at four schools in my rural NC school district is that I could not spend more time with every student who needed my help. Accurate ELL identification is one way of ensuring that ESL services can appropriately reach every student who needs them.

5.3 What Teachers Should Know About Hispanicized English(es)

If I could sum up the features I wish teachers knew about HE, I would turn to the three 'Myths and Realities' located in a dialect curriculum created by researchers at North Carolina State University (Reaser and Wolfram 2007; Askin 2008). The resources in this curriculum help both students and teachers understand vital facts about language variation (the ideas covered in section 4.1) in terms of dialects from many areas of NC. The curriculum can be accessed online and is free to use. The discussion in this section is adapted from Askin (2008) and material in the dialect curriculum.

> MYTH 1: *Hispanic varieties of English are simply derived from imperfect learning and/or Spanish language transfer.*

This myth characterizes Hispanicized English as just 'English with a Spanish accent.' Only second-language speakers of English speak HE, the thinking goes. Speakers are trying to pronounce their words the way monolingual (Standard) English speakers do—and fail—because they are still learning English.

In reality, Latino/Hispanic/Chicano varieties of English have their own 'accent' patterns, just the way New York English, Southern Englishes and British Englishes do. Speakers of these varieties may, like speakers of these varieties of US English, be monolingual in English. Many will know Spanish to varying degrees and increasing numbers of them will only be able to understand Spanish (e.g., have 'receptive proficiency'), not speak it. NCHE is, in short, its own dialect. It has its own sound, word and sentence patterns that are independent from those of English *or* Spanish as well as contributions from both languages.

> MYTH 2: *Spanish is new in the US.*

The first permanent settlement, in 1492, in what is now the US, in St. Augustine, was Spanish speaking. Later, Spanish explorers conquered areas that are now the states of New Mexico and Utah. California, Nevada, Colorado and Texas/Tejas (all Spanish words) were Spanish speaking before they were English speaking. Thus, there was a Spanish-speaking presence in the US long before the early 19th century, when the aforementioned states were incorporated into the US Hispanic people, like indigenous/Native American people, were regional "Americans" long before Europeans. The historical legacy of Spanish survives prominently in the traditions, architecture, food, music, culture, art and language of the American West and Southwest—and it is now a distinct part of our own national character.

MYTH 3: *Spanish is a threat to English* (Reaser and Wolfram 2007; Askin 2008).

Though many people think that English's status as the most prominent language of the US is being challenged by Spanish, this fact is not borne out in reality—in NC or in most immigrant communities in the US. In fact, most immigrant (home) languages are lost after three generations. The classic model for language shift over generations of immigrant language looks like this:

Generation 1 (immigrants): Spanish only
Generation 2 (native born): Bilingual/Spanish and English
Generation 3 (native born): English only

In North Carolina, this shift has happened in many places in *two* generations—the first generation of immigrants learned (some) English very quickly and their children may not have much maintained Spanish at all (Reaser et al. 2017). This new generation of speakers has, however, formed their own dialect of English: NCHE. It differs in distinct ways from other regional varieties of Latino/Chicano Englishes like those spoken in Miami (which has a large Cuban population) or New York City (which has a large Puerto Rican population). Just as you can tell where someone's from in the US by the way they speak (for example, "he's from up North," "She must be from the South"), some speakers of NCHE could tell you fairly easily, "That new student is from Los Angeles"—just by the way the 'new student' sounds when s/he speaks English!

In fact, it can be very hard, even for trained linguists, to tell whether NCHE speakers are bilingual at all! I have given the following 'quiz' (*bilingual or not?*) to many undergraduate and graduate classes over the years with varying levels of linguistics training—and no one has ever gotten all the questions 'right.' You can take the quiz too. The sound clip located at the following link, which plays eight speech samples of Hispanicized English in NC, contains both monolingual (English-only) and bilingual (Spanish/English) varieties of English. Each clip is repeated twice. Your job is to guess whether the speaker is bilingual or not:

https://languageandlife.org/vonc/vonc35.mp4

As it turns out, half of the speakers from the audio clip speak English only (Speakers 1, 3, 5 and 6) and the other half are bilingual (Speakers 2, 4, 7 and 8). You can watch a brief video vignette from the NC State Dialect Curriculum on *Spanish in NC* at the following link:

https://languageandlife.org/vonc/vonc36.mp4

5.4   In Closing: *El que sabe dos idiomas . . .*

There is a popular saying, in the field of bilingual education and beyond: *El que sabe dos idiomas vale por dos* ('He who speaks two languages is worth two'). My goal as a teacher-educator is that all teacher candidates become both practically and academically 'bilingual': in both the language of the classroom (a process that takes many years, if not decades to fully acquire), but also in the language of academic research—in terms of a rigorous understandings of language acquisition, linguistics and language variation. We can best help our students learn new things if we know how and why they know what they do. My hope is that this chapter, and this volume, has been a small step in helping a process of professional 'bilingualism' grow—for students like *Marcos*.

Notes

1. As of 2008, the NC Department of Public Instruction had transitioned to using the WIDA Access Placement Test (W-APT).
2. The NC Public Schools publication, *Guidelines for testing students identified as limited English proficient*, notes that schools may consult with a parent or guardian to consider whether the HLS was completed correctly. In my experience, many parents of NCHE speakers were not fluent in spoken English, nor literate in English—and, practically speaking, the budget for interpreters was limited to more formal events (e.g., parent-teacher conferences, IEP (Individual Education Plan) meetings (mandated by the Federal Individuals with Disabilities Act)).
3. As of 2005, the NC State Board of Education set a goal that all long-term LEP students in NC Public Schools would be exited after five years ("By the 2013–2014 academic year, 100 percent of students identified as limited English proficient and who have been in U.S. schools for at least five years shall score at the Superior level on all subtests of the State-identified English language proficiency test" (NC Department of Public Instruction 2005: 7)). In my anecdotal experience, one or two K-12 students of the 60 or so in my caseload exited the ESL program each year.
4. Another widely used language proficiency test, the Woodcook-Muñoz Language Survey (WMLS), indicated that *none* of the native English-speaking students in Pray's (2005) study were proficient in English.
5. Mallinson and Charity Hudley (2011) note that passage-independent questions (e.g., "What did you eat for lunch?"), which rely on students' preexisting personal knowledge, are more accurate indicators of reading comprehension than passage-dependent questions ("What did the girl in the story eat for lunch?").
6. The 1974 US Supreme Court decision in *Lau v. Nichols* ensured that all language learners in US schools, under the provisions of section 601 of the Civil Rights Act of 1964, receive educational and language support. Today, all US school districts are responsible for demonstrating their fulfillment of these requirements (e.g., by providing ESL services to qualified students).

References

Askin, H. 2008. Spanish and hispanic English in North Carolina. LEARN NC. University of North Carolina School of Education. Retrieved 8/6/17 from <www.learnnc.org/lp/pages/4831>.

Ballard, W. S., E. F. Dalton, and P. L. Tighe. 1995. *IDEA oral language proficiency test in English* (5th ed.). Los Angeles: Ballard and Tighe. Google Scholar.

Fasold, R. W., W. Labov, F. B. Vaughn-Cooke, G. Bailey, W. Wolfram, A. K. Spears, and J. Rickford. 1987. Are black and white vernaculars diverging? Papers from the NWAVE XIV panel discussion. *American Speech 62.1*: 3–80.

Figueroa, R. A. 1990. Best practices in the assessment of bilingual children. In Thomas, A. and J. Grimes (eds.), *Best practices in school psychology*: 93–106. Washington, DC: National Association of School Psychologists.

Fought, C. 2003. *Chicano English in context*. Basingstoke, UK: Palgrave.

Geisinger, K. F., and J. Carlson. 1992. *Assessing language-minority students*. ERIC Document Reproduction Service No. ED356232.

Hernández, R. D. 1994. Reducing bias in the assessment of culturally and linguistically diverse populations. *The Journal of Educational Issues of Language Minority Students 14*: 269–300.

Kendall, T. 2007. The North Carolina sociolinguistic archive and analysis project: Empowering the sociolinguistic archive. *Penn Working Papers in Linguistics 13.2*: 15–26. Philadelphia: University of Pennsylvania.

Labov, W. 1972. *Language in the Inner City: Studies in the black English Vernacular*. Philadelphia: University of Pennsylvania Press.

Labov, W. 1994. *Principles of linguistic change*. Volume 1: Internal factors. Oxford: Blackwell.

Linguistic Society of America. 1997. Resolution on the 'Ebonics' issue. Annual Meeting of the Linguistic Society of America, Chicago, IL: 1/97.

Matteson, B. 2013. NC General Assembly Fiscal Research Division. Funding of North Carolina's Public Schools. Presentation to Joint Appropriations Subcommittee on Education. North Carolina General Assembly. 2/2013. Retrieved from <http://legislative.ncpublicschools.gov/committee-presentations/2013-committee-presentations/20130219-fiscalpres-psfunding.pdf>.

North Carolina Department of Public Instruction. 2005. *Guidelines for testing students identified as limited English proficient*. NC Testing Program, Grades 3–12. Raleigh, NC: State Board of Education Department of Public Instruction: Division of Accountability Services/North Carolina Testing Program. Retrieved from <www.dpi.state.nc.us/docs/accountability/policyoperations/LEPGuidelines_Sept05.pdf> on 9/14/2017.

North Carolina Department of Public Instruction. 2008. Sample North Carolina Home Language Survey Form. Retrieved from NC Wise Owl <http://esl.ncwiseowl.org/UserFiles/Servers/Server_4502383/File/SAMPLE%20North%20Carolina%20Home%20Language%20Survey%20Form.doc> on 10/12/2017.

Reaser, J. C., C. Temple Adger, W. Wolfram, and D. Christian. 2017. *Dialects at school: Education linguistically diverse students*. New York: Routledge.

Reaser, J. C., and W. Wolfram. 2007. *Voices of North Carolina: Language and life from the Atlantic to the Appalachians*. North Carolina State University. Retrieved 10/14/2017 from <https://linguistics.chass.ncsu.edu/thinkanddo/vonc.php>.

Steele, C. M., and J. Aronson. 1995. Stereotype vulnerability and the intellectual test performance of African Americans. *Journal of Personality and Social Psychology* 69: 797–811.

Appendix A
English Proficiency Level Descriptions

English Proficiency Levels	Novice Low	Novice High	Intermediate Low
Listening	No functional ability in understanding spoken English.	Understands simple questions and statements on familiar topics if spoken very slowly and distinctly; often requires restatement in graphic terms.	Understands most questions, statements and conversations on familiar topics spoken distinctly at normal speed; requires occasional restatement.
Speaking	No functional ability in speaking English.	Able to satisfy routine daily speaking needs. Can ask and answer questions on very familiar topics. Speaking vocabulary is inadequate to express anything but the most elementary needs. Should be able to follow simple classroom directions.	Can handle with confidence but not facility most daily speaking situations. Can handle limited scholastic language requirements; will need help for most tasks. Limited vocabulary often reduces the students to verbal groping or momentary silence.
Writing	No functional ability in writing English.	Able to copy isolated words or short phrases. Can write simple, memorized material with frequent misspellings and inaccuracies.	Sufficient control of writing system to meet some survival needs. Able to compose short paragraphs or take simple notes on very familiar topics grounded in personal experience. Evidence of good control of basic sentence construction and inflections such as subject/verb agreement; and straightforward syntactic constructions in present, past and future time though errors occasionally occur.

English Proficiency Levels	Novice Low	Novice High	Intermediate Low
Reading	No functional ability in reading English.	Reads and understands simple narrative and descriptive text. Vocabulary for comprehension is limited to simple elementary needs such as names, addresses, dates, short informative signs (e.g., street signs, no smoking, exit). Material understood rarely exceeds a single phrase and comprehension requires rereading and checking. Can recognize all letters in the alphabet. Detail is overlooked or misunderstood.	Sufficient comprehension to understand simple material. Can read messages, greetings, popular advertising, letters and invitations. Can guess at unfamiliar vocabulary if highly contextualized. Understands short discourse on familiar topics. Misinterpretation still occurs with more complex material. May have to read material several times.

English Proficiency Levels	Intermediate High	Advanced	Superior
Listening	Understands most informal questions, statements and conversations at normal speed; comprehends lectures on familiar subjects with some difficulty.	Understands most conversations and most lectures on familiar subjects at normal speed.	Understands academic topical conversations and most lectures with no difficulty.
Speaking	Participates effectively, sometimes hesitatingly, in social and academic conversations; makes occasional errors in idiom and structure, often obscuring meaning.	Able to speak the language in most situations. Comprehension is quite complete for a normal rate of speech. Makes occasional errors in idiom and structure that obscure meaning.	Able to use language fluently on all levels, normal to school-related needs. Can understand and participate in almost any conversation within the range of experience with a high degree of fluency.

English Proficiency Levels	Intermediate High	Advanced	Superior
Writing	Sufficient control of writing system to meet most survival needs. Can take notes in some detail on familiar topics and respond to personal questions using elementary vocabulary and common structures. Can express rather accurately present and future time. Can produce some past verb forms, but not always accurately or with correct usage.	Can write simple social correspondence, take notes, write summaries, and describe factual topics. Still makes common errors in spelling and punctuation but shows some control of the most common conventions. Able to join sentences in limited discourse, but has difficulty in producing complex sentences. Paragraphs are reasonably unified and coherent.	Able to use the written language effectively in most exchanges. Can write short papers and express statements of position, points of view and arguments. Good control of structure, spelling and vocabulary. Can use complex and compound sentence structures to express ideas clearly and coherently. Still has problem tailoring writing to a variety of audiences and styles.
Reading	Able to read simple printed material within a familiar context. Can read uncomplicated prose on familiar subjects in frequently used sentence patterns. Some misunder-standings. Able to read the facts but cannot draw inferences.	Sufficient comprehension to understand most factual information in nontechnical prose as well as some discussions on concrete topics related to special interests. Able to read for information and description, to follow sequence of events, and to react to that information. Able to separate main ideas from lesser ones and to use that division to advance understanding. Can locate and interpret main ideas and details in material written for the general public.	Able to read standard newspaper items addressed to the general reader, routine correspondence reports and technical material in a field of interest at a normal rate of speed. Can gain new knowledge from material on unfamiliar topics in areas of a general nature. Can interpret hypotheses, supported opinions and conjectures. Able to read between the lines. May be unable to appreciate nuance or style.

Index

Note: Page numbers in *italics* denote references to Figures and page numbers in **bold** denote references to Tables.